# AN ARKANSAS CHILDHOOD

*For Ruth & Jud & Judith & Bill*

*with my deepest love,*

*Margaret Walker*

# An
# Arkansas
# Childhood

## Growing Up in the
## Athens of the Ozarks

### Margaret Mullen

**m & m PRESS**
Fayetteville, Arkansas

AN ARKANSAS CHILDHOOD

First Edition published 1989

ISBN 0-943099-06-4

A gift of love

to

Michael and Sally

In memory of

James Ralph Jewell
Edna Keith Jewell
James Ralph Jewell, Jr.

# ACKNOWLEDGMENTS

My deep gratitude goes to my children for understanding my need to write; to the teachers: Nancy Sully, Frances Mayes, Dick Maxwell, Burghild Holzer, Mary Jane Moffat, and James Fetler, who have encouraged me as I learned to write; and to the friends and fellow students who have listened to and critiqued many of these episodes.

Certain of the episodes have been previously printed in *Coast Light, Across the Generations, Fresh Hot Bread,* and in the quarterly of the Washington County Historical Society, *Flashback.* My thanks to them.

# Contents

# *One*

# Home in Emporia

## *The Shimmer of Memory*

**M**Y WISH to record the exceedingly happy memories of my childhood comes as sort of a support system, I suppose—proof of part of my life that was idyllic or that seems so in memory. Understanding now more than I could have as a child, girl, and young woman, I realize some of the effort it must have taken by my parents to make their children's childhood so free, secure, and stimulating. True, the times were a bit different. Perhaps the shimmer of memory colors this picture too brightly, glosses over the shadows. But I try to be honest, and what fictionalizing I do is an attempt to faithfully record the truth of feeling if not always of fact.

Some parts of life go on and on in endless repetition; others develop and change, growing into different entities (metamorphosis being one of our eternal mysteries). Times and people vanish. Only our memories hold the originals, recalling them to validate our own experience.

My children flourished in suburban California and I reveled in the freedoms permitted them, but, at the same time, I yearned for certain different freedoms of my youth, gone forever it seemed. My yearning triggered memories and the desire to capture such memories in words so that they might not vanish from a busy world.

Born in a small town in Kansas—Emporia, the home of William Allen White, eminent journalist and author,

1

who was an older friend and mentor of my father—I lived as the eldest child in a small family that was stable, happy, and bound very closely one to the other. My parents had been childhood sweethearts and built a marriage that lasted for more than fifty-five years. I well remember the celebration of my paternal grandparents' Golden Wedding and confidently expected such a family pattern to be my own. Life and death intervened.

I enjoyed the casually sheltered, paradoxically independent life of a "faculty brat" on the campus of Kansas State Normal School and later the University of Arkansas. My father had done his graduate work in psychology with G. Stanley Hall at Clark University and was delighted to have a child of his own to watch develop and experiment with. It made for an unusually stimulating childhood. Our parents loved us deeply and were, at the same time, greatly interested in us as people. We had astonishing freedom balanced by strict personal accountability.

Four and a half years younger than I, my brother Jimmie was born shortly before we left Kansas to move to the Ozarks—Fayetteville, Arkansas—where my father was to become dean of the newly created College of Education at the University. A baby sister, Keith Coe, born when I was eleven and given family names in the Southern tradition, was part of our family for less than four years, dying of bulbar polio in Tennessee, where we were visiting cousins of my father.

The personal privacy accorded each member of my intimate family amazes me. We children were far enough apart in age and interests that we had different circles of friends and fields of activity. Although we did many things together as a family, my brother and I had to wait for a real friendship until we had a year together at college.

It was an idyllic world for me, filled with ample space both indoors and out to do what interested me most: run, read, climb trees, jump rope, roller skate, play dolls, dress up, or lie on the grass and dream for hours on end. And there was time—running on and on, bound by day and night and mealtimes but little else. True, we were in church and Sunday School each Sunday, as were my friends, and during the week I went to school, but school was an experimental one on the campus, actually in the same building, first floor, as my father's offices, second floor. I attended that same school until I entered college—on that same Arkansas campus. School seemed as natural to me as breathing until my actual registration as a freshman. At that point I became as "green" as any other new student, terrified of doing something wrong. My terror was perhaps heightened by the years I had spent since infancy watching and admiring the college students who appeared to me to be profoundly mature and sophisticated.

The focus of this group of memories is only on the earliest part of my life and runs only long enough to record our important move across the Mason Dixon line (in my childhood still an immensely important boundary). My world at that time held, in addition to my immediate family, my paternal grandparents, the cousins, aunts and uncles of my parents, who were only children, our friends and our cooks and hired help—also friends. It was a close and lovely world.

### October Fourth

*The afternoon before my birth*
*we walked together, the three of us*
*through the gold autumn.*
*My father set the pace*
*brown hair blown by the breeze,*
*eyeglasses shining in the sun,*
*careful not to hurry my mother,*
*shorter and heavy with me—*
*to be their first born.*
*Against a clean blue Kansas sky,*
*butter-yellow cottonwoods*
*had already lost early leaves,*
*rising thinly now in smoke*
*from pungent bonfires.*
*It was a day, they said,*
*for dreaming.*

*Rocked in my safest cradle, I knew*
*happiness early, hungered for vision*
*and the fragrances of fall.*
*The pulse of my mother's heart*
*quickened with my readiness.*

## Home in Emporia

The ample Victorian house where I was born and lived the first five years of my life had room, it seemed, for everything. Surrounded by a wide veranda, it stood six or seven steps above the front walk, facing a much larger home across a wide grassy stretch big enough for still another house. There were narrow flower beds below the porch where my mother planted bulbs and fought an unequal battle with poison ivy.

When you came in the front door from the veranda, you were in a small entry facing a short wall on which hung a glowing pastel of Venice mounted on gold board and framed in gold. It was to me the most beautiful picture in the world and the take-off point for endless dreams. Turning to the left through a wide arch, you entered a long, wood-paneled living room/library lined with bookshelves. Memory fails to tell me about the furnishings except for a high-backed caned rocker, my mother's, and a comfortable, reclining Morris chair, my father's. I had my own small rocker. It was a room in which people sat to read and talk. Before I can remember most other details, I can go back to the feeling of wanting to read, hoping to find out what excitement, what charm lay in the objects called books. I was surrounded by them always. Walls, more often than not, supported bookcases. Books lay on tables, on chairs, were even stacked on the floor in library and living room. My parents held me and showed me the right side up of pictures and how to turn the pages so they wouldn't tear. They read to me and to each other from these ever-present books and papers.

At the far end of the living room was a sliding door to the dining room. More nearly square than the living room, it provided room for a big round table that could expand, forever in my eyes, with the addition of heavy leaves. A ponderous buffet held down one wall, a china cabinet stood between windows, and six or eight chairs were placed at the table or against the walls.

One went to the kitchen through another swinging door, to the left as one entered from the living room. I remember it as always bright and sunny—perhaps because I was too young to see it in the busy evening hours. There was a highly polished coal range, a sink under windows that again looked across the broad lawn, many cabinets for the china Mother loved, a small table and chairs. Mrs. Washington, a handsome middle-aged black woman, ruled the kitchen and was a lovingly regarded friend and advisor to the young family. Her husband (she did not live in) was a great hunter and fisherman. It was he who had supplied the 'possum for a festive party my parents gave that featured this unusual entree. My parents enjoyed entertaining. Running into the kitchen that day to show off my "dress-up" costume—a moss-green basque of ribbed silk, heavily embroidered and touched with dull gold, a favorite of my mother's—I interrupted a family council about the timing of the roast. My father swung me off my feet, lifted me over his head and, calling me his "little gypsy," twirled around and around while my brown curls lifted and my heart nearly stopped with joy.

I was told the next day that the 'possum tasted like roast pig—"very fat." The morsel given to me to taste was a crackling bit of skin.

If you had turned to the right on entering from the front door, you found yourself in a little parlor, small and rather uninteresting, I thought, because no games were played there. Only adults dressed in their finest seemed to find pleasure in sitting there, talking to each other. I was not encouraged to handle the beautiful objects in a glass case or on the tables. A hallway separated the living room and parlor and gave access from parlor to dining room. Stairs rose from the end of the hall to the second floor.

Our bedrooms were there, as well as an all-purpose sewing and guest room, all lit by wide windows through which we could see the maples, elms, and cottonwoods close to the house and the broad fields in the distance. I have a hazy memory of a slow stream some distance away, tall sycamores lining its banks. I could only have walked there with my parents.

Our maid jumped out of the sewing room window one night and fell into the rosebushes below. She had been left to tend me (an infant less than a year old) while my parents attended some campus function. When they returned home earlier than expected, she feared intruders and abandoned me to leap out of the window in her absolute panic. The story was told over and over, and I'm afraid that my parents' compassion for her deep scratches and sprained ankle was considerably tempered by their feeling that she should not have left me to cope alone with the possible invaders.

Leading up to the attic was a narrow, closed stairway, entered through a door, ordinarily closed, beside the sewing room. I had to ask permission to go to the attic and most often went there with my mother, smelling the dry, clean dust, leaning out miniature windows under the eaves, and marveling at how different the world looked from such a height. Old books have a special fragrance that changes in sunshine or rain. Breathing deeply I can still resurrect the mix of yellowed pages, leather bindings, mustiness, printer's ink, and the particular dust of bookshelves. The floor was made of smooth, wide boards, only loosely nailed to the girders. Light fell on them slantwise from the low windows and dust motes danced in the slanting rays.

Although excitement lay in the trunks and boxes from which "dress-up" clothes sometimes came and I liked to look at the quaint advertisements in the crisp, yellowed newspapers that covered the boxes and barrels, I was always impatient to get to the octagonal room in the cupola. Sometimes I was allowed to stay there alone after Mother finished her attic errand. There were windows all around over a narrow window seat, and under the seat were two wide shelves. They were packed tight with books, retired or surplus from the downstairs shelves: delicate novels in pastel Victorian bindings (violets, roses, lilacs, and daisies bloomed singly or in garlands and bouquets on the covers; one book was all in ivy—green and fresh), my parents' old school books, heavy brown and gold volumes often in sets. The old copies of the *National Geographic* were stored there before binding, as well as *Collier's, The American Magazine*, the *Literary Digest*, and *The Saturday Evening Post*. It was a place of endless delight to me.

I had been "reading" since I was big enough to hold a book, and I'm not sure when the printed symbols began to have their own real meaning for me. The story is that for a long time my biggest problem was in crossing my legs. I was a chubby child, and my short, fat, three or four-year-old legs would not stay one over the other in the stylish adult posture I admired in my parents. Downstairs in the living room, in my white rocker, I had to pay a great deal of attention to my troublesome legs. I tugged and pulled, and sometimes Mother or Daddy would help me achieve the desired position. Then the top leg would slide off and I would have to start all over again. In the attic there was no problem. There were no chairs. I sat cross-legged on the floor or lay on my stomach on the window seat, pulled out book after book, sniffed the dry air, and tasted heaven.

Our home in Emporia was to be our haven for a much shorter time than I could have dreamed. I have

never gone back except in memory, but that has sufficed
to keep it glowing and alive in my mind and heart.

## Daddy

Daddy's love of storytelling continued throughout his
life. He sent outrageous tales home from college in his
letters, identified by little printed tabs saying, "Joke,"
and he created fiction of his own, as when he mailed a
discarded cicada shell east to a friend in Massachusetts.
The carefully wrapped package bore the label,
"Warning—Kansas chigger inside. Do not release." His
friend, slow to reply, finally reported that fortunately the
insect seemed to have died en route but that he had had
no idea that chiggers were so large!

My father's popularity as a public speaker came
about, I'm sure, because of his basic love of people and
his ability to stimulate and engage their interest. Using
his stories as bait, he was able to deliver a powerful message that was not forgotten when the laughter ceased. A
great crusader for education, he was in demand all over
the country for single speeches, Lyceum Series,
teachers' institutes, and what are now called mini-
courses.

And how he loved to teach! A devotee of the Socratic
method, he had a class in the palm of his hand before
they knew it. He used devices, now touted as "new methods of interpersonal evaluation" to engage students in
the recognition and ranking of their own values. No
class ended without heated discussion, and all of his
classes were filled to standing room. At the U of A a
required class for freshmen intending to become

teachers carried the nondescript title, "Introduction to Education." It regularly enrolled such campus leaders as Bill Fulbright, who took it as a senior. A lowly freshman who had to take it, even if her father taught the course, I was thrilled to be seated behind Bill's handsome head.

A good many of my father's pupils and friends made their way into public service, and they kept in touch over the years. Brooks Hayes, a Representative from Arkansas, who became an advisor to President Kennedy, and Jim Trimble, another Congressman, were among these U of A alumni.

As a student himself in September 1899, Daddy entered Coe College in Cedar Rapids, Iowa. This small liberal arts college had been founded in 1853 after a gift of land, "a quarter section," by his grandfather, Daniel Coe. It was to be a hard struggle financially. Although he had been engaged in various money-making enterprises in high school and one year at Highland Academy, the bank in Moran, Kansas, to which he had entrusted his savings, failed in 1898, taking with it not only his college funds but the whole of the family fortune—meager as it was.

Not daunted by this misadventure, Daddy got a job in the Coe College printing office and started "hashing" in a popular downtown restaurant. At Christmas time, he got a job in the post office. He stayed in Cedar Rapids that summer to work there and continued to be employed whenever the post office put on extra help.

But by the spring of 1901, Daddy had to leave Coe and go to work full time, his finances entirely exhausted. He had worked nights for the *Cedar Rapids Republican* while going to classes in the daytime and working for the post office when not in class. Now he was given a desk as telegraph editor for the *Republican* and received the princely salary of fifteen dollars a week. Daddy continued at the paper for the next year, and although he became assistant city editor, his proud boast in later years was of his official Printers' Union card, a union notoriously "hard to crack."

In the summer of 1902, he crammed on academic work in order to take advanced standing examinations that would permit him to re-enter Coe in the fall with his class. This he did, carrying a double major in psychology and English. In June, 1903, the faculty elected him valedictorian after a serious discussion over his eligibility—he had been out of college for a year and a half!

My father had the help of college authorities and Dr. Carl Seashore of Iowa State University in receiving a graduate fellowship from Clark University in Worcester, Massachusetts. There he worked for his Ph.D. in psychology with G. Stanley Hall, the eminent psychologist and president of Clark at the time. Although his fellowship made it financially possible for him to pursue his graduate work, it provided little else. He recorded $23.68 as his total expenses for March of 1904. Of that, ten dollars went to pay for his room and one dollar for a gallery ticket to hear Nordica sing in *Parsifal*.

He had entered a world of cultural opportunity unknown to Moran or Cedar Rapids, and for the rest of his life delighted in music, both opera and concert hall, and in theater. In November he heard *Parsifal* again, doing without dinner for a couple of days in order to pay for a ticket.

Later, during my childhood, Daddy was an enthusiastic supporter of the Fayetteville Lyceum and of the university's performance program. As Director of the Summer Session, he brought the Ben Greet Players, an English Shakespearean troupe, to present a season of six or eight comedies and tragedies in an outdoor theater under the trees that shaded Senior Walk. I first saw *As*

*You Like It* there, *Midsummer Night's Dream*, *King Lear*, *The Merchant of Venice*.

We were taken to the St. Louis Symphony with Rudolph Ganz conducting, to Syd Chaplin in *Charley's Aunt*. The Tony Sarg marionettes excited my fancy in the *Willow Plate Story*; Judge Ben Linley and John Cowper Powys spoke on the Lecture Series. We heard Sousa and his famous band, Don Jose Mujica (whose dark eyes and soaring tenor made impressionable female students spend many a sleepless night), saw the Coffer-Miller Players in *The Rivals* and never missed a D'Oyle Carte, Gilbert and Sullivan production of *The Mikado*, *Pirates of Penzance*, or *Pinafore*. We drove home after such treats with Daddy singing his favorite parts and later listened to the Victrola rendition of "Buttercup," "Three Little Maids," or whatever other selection we chose. "I am the very model of a modern major general" was a great favorite.

When we lived in Emporia, Daddy was very active in amateur theatricals and, among other roles, sang the part of Gaspard the miser in *The Chimes of Normandy*. The *Emporia Gazette* reported that "Gaspard was the star last night. No better production has ever been given in Kansas." Suffice it to say that while the realism of the scene so frightened my four-year-old friend, De Witt Williams, that he screamed when he thought my father was about to be attacked, I sensed the total drama of the stage and was half-way down the aisle to join the players before my embarrassed mother could catch me and take me back to our seats.

My father's years at Clark were rich in friends and new experiences but also in academic stimulation. He wrote a master's thesis on "Foreign School Systems" while doing an article on the "Psychology of Dreams" that was accepted for his eventual doctoral dissertation. He had sent out more than fifty letters to European

Ministers of Agriculture asking for data on Agricultural Education. Perhaps in recognition of his varied interests, he was named Senior Fellow. Then he undertook a second doctoral thesis using and amplifying the information received from his foreign inquiries. The reply from Russia turned out to be the first official material ever elicited from that source. This thesis was later published by the United States Bureau of Education, exhausting a supply of 60,000 copies, and became the basis for the structure of the Smith-Hughes Act. As if this were not enough to fill his time, he proofed the entire two volume classic, *Adolescence*, by Dr. Hall, tutored in French and German for his orals, and presented a highly praised abstract of Lay's *Experimentelle Didaktik*.

Finally, after these intense years, he was ready to seek a teaching position. After a couple of false starts, he went to the Southwest Louisiana Industrial Institute in Lafayette as Director of Teacher Training. The salary was $1,200 a year. Daddy found a kindred soul in President Stephens, who shared his delight in nonsense rhymes and named him editor of the *Louisiana School Review*. It was a happy year, capped with his assignment as Acting President for the summer, when he also organized, administered, and taught in the first summer session of the institution.

My father's year in Louisiana gave him some gustatory pleasures that he had not known before, and for the rest of his life he was to send regularly to a specialty shop in New Orleans for a particular kind of chicory that he used sparingly in brewing the coffee of which he was so fond. His gourmet tastes often taxed his limited budget and eventually led to the cooperative buying project through which he brought Baltimore oysters, Seattle halibut and salmon, New Orleans shrimp, Michigan celery, Ohio honey, and California Tokay grapes to his and his friends' dining tables in Fayetteville, Arkansas.

But between Louisiana and Arkansas came six years in Emporia, Kansas, where he was on the faculty of the Kansas State Normal School (KSN, for short) teaching psychology and general education courses. This job offered the opportunity for Daddy to stabilize plans for the wedding he and my mother had impatiently postponed since their engagement nine years before, on August 27, 1898, when my father was twenty, my mother eighteen. My parents had been schoolmates, sweethearts since childhood, and after a certain fifteenth birthday party of my mother's on January 12, 1895, Daddy decided that she was to be "his girl" for all time. They gave each other valentines the following month and mutual devotion the rest of their lives.

## Best Friends

Parents always seem old to their children. I would never have known the young, giddy side of my mother if we had not made those treasured trips to the minute town in Kansas where my parents had grown up as childhood sweethearts and where Grandma and Grandpa, my father's parents, still lived. Always during those visits, Mother set aside an overnight stay with her best friend, Edith Strong. "Aunt Edith" was nearly a year older than Mother, but she had never married and ran the inherited family farm with skill and enjoyment. She was tall, round-bosomed, and had brown hair that frizzled at her temples. Most of life's minor problems she met with a high-pitched giggly laugh. I was usually taken on these visits to "The Farm" until I got too big for it to be fun and my brother went along to take my place.

Out to the farm we went, and from the time they laid eyes on each other the talking never stopped. "Remember when. . . ?" would set off a torrent of giggles that broke into helpless laughter again and again. Mealtimes lasted forever and conventional manners were forgotten. There were always new kittens, a puppy or two, small fluffy chicks and ducklings to keep me busy. Sometimes I could gather eggs or go down to the barn to watch Walter, the hired man, milk.

But the real excitement was to see my mother race laughing to the swing or jump to hang from the low branch of a tree. To see her long hair loose and flying was like a dream. And, most of all, when I lay in the very middle of the huge feather bed and watched my mother and her best friend get ready for the night, put on billowing night dresses, brush each other's hair, and come to lie, one on each side of me, as they talked and giggled on into the night, I knew unbelievable rapture.

## Home Again

We'd been in Colorado for the summer, my last one as an "only" because my brother was to be born the following February, expanding our family to four. Our cabin, perched on a steep slope above Green Mountain Falls, opened its back door against the mountainside. It took twenty-two steps from the rocky ground to reach the balcony-like front porch. I knew very well how many steps there were, because I insisted on climbing them to wash my hands in a shallow enamel basin whenever I played in the clear mountain stream that splashed over the stony creek bed at the foot of the steps. My fixation on hand-washing was a source of wonder and amusement to my parents, but I made it clear that it was a necessity to me. It had something to do, I remember, with "cleaning-up" after being outdoors. Not quite four years old and apparently deaf to reason, I toiled up and down the stairs, alternately paddling in the crystal stream and stirring up Ivory suds in the basin set on the porch floor. First warm water and then icy cold—it felt good but I got very tired.

When I abandoned my water sports, I could go for the mail, down the narrow mountain path to ask the post-mistress if the mail had come. She peered down from behind her wicket. I tilted my head way back and stretched to see her. I was blissfully ignorant at the time that the LONG walk was far less than a block and could be observed over its entire length by my parents, sitting on the front porch of our cabin. No one could have felt more the adventurer than I, or further from surveil-lance!

An old sepia snapshot from that summer shows me sun-burned and wide-eyed under a cartwheel sailor hat, which I thought was patent leather. It must have been some kind of shiny oilcloth. Mother and Daddy assured me that they watched for that hat so they would know that I was on my way home. What a gift of freedom they made me!

The endless summer ended, and we traveled on the train back to Kansas, probably on the old Katy (M, K & T—Missouri, Kansas and Texas) that ran through Emporia. A polished Model T taxi took us home, and the small, world-weary traveler I was then rested one foot up on the veranda step, yawned, and sighed, "Finally—home again!"

## The Doll

Mary Rebecca Coe—a proper name—legacy from my grandmother, loved and revered, expert in kindness, one who allowed no harm to come to those she loved. Her name insurance for present and future safety—surely nothing but good could come to Mary Rebecca Coe!

The first doll to come after dolls became people, discovered under cushions in a Pullman compartment, hidden there by a kindly porter on instructions from my parents, hoping to tempt me toward future travel. China head with painted black curls, china hands and neatly booted feet, soft cloth body, arms and legs attached. Come from an earlier age than mine to be my friend, companion, name-sake guardian.

Yet one hot day as I held her by the hand, spinning round and about in my own breeze to escape the summer heat, she left me—arm pulled from body by a force I could not understand, china head broken as it hit the wall.

Mary Rebecca Coe, the unconquerable, conquered and gone.

## The Money Store

Judge Parker was a community leader, a federal judge and a highly respected man. To me, all this couldn't have mattered less. At almost four, I knew him as a friend of my father's but nearly as old as my grandfather. He was not tall but carried himself as if he were, with a trim erectness and a direct gaze that seemed to respect me as highly as it did my elders. I loved him—

perhaps the first man outside my family about  whom I could say that.

And he seemed to return my affection. When we met walking across the campus or on a downtown street, he would greet my parents and then bend down and swing me up to hold me face to face with him as he asked, "What makes Margaret so heavy?" My answer, reflecting my parents' enjoyment of language, was always, "Big vocabulary makes Margaret heavy." I had no idea why Mother and Daddy and Judge Parker laughed so hard at this until much later in my life, but I was happy to have pleased them.

More times than not, the judge set me down on my feet, took my hand, and asked in a serious manner, "Do you think we could persuade your parents to have a dish of ice cream?" Sometimes the answer was a heartbreaking "No," but often they smiled "Yes," and we walked off to The Money Store.

This was not a bank but an old-fashioned confectionery with round walnut tables supported by curving black wire legs and walnut seated chairs where the wires twisted up from the legs to make heart-shaped backs. There were long, polished mirrors behind glass cases that displayed confections beyond counting: marzipan fruits, chocolate drops, creamy white divinity dotted with nuts, thick chocolate fudge, red-striped peppermints, and pink wintergreen lozenges prominent among them.

We would enter in what I considered great style, and Judge Parker would seat me as my father seated my mother. Only three flavors were offered in ice cream: vanilla, chocolate, and strawberry, but I was always asked by my host as solicitously as if it were the first time and the choices were many. I always chose chocolate. When we finished the cool treat and the two thin sugar wafers served with it—Clover Leaves they were

called—Judge Parker would speak quietly to our waitress as she handed him the check and then give her a
bill. She always nodded, went away, and when she came
back she sometimes gave him a bill that looked just like
the one he had given her, but then she would come
'round and give me real money. I realize now that it
probably never exceeded a quarter, but it was in many
pieces—pennies, a nickel or two, sometimes a dime
(which felt thin and insignificant to me). My mother frequently shook her head and said, "Oh, Judge Parker. . ."
This was beyond my understanding, but he always
replied, "That's what happens at the money store." And
then we would thank the waitress and go out.

## Homecoming Queen

In 1912, the autumn I was four, I was old enough, I
felt, to be quite a person, not yet threatened by the advent
of my younger brother. And that was the fall I ruled as
Homecoming Queen.

Emporia supported two colleges, Kansas State
Normal School, where my father taught, and the College
of Emporia, which my mother had attended. I can remember spirited arguments about the superiority of one
or the other, always ending in gales of laughter. The
football team of neither ever made sporting history, I'm
sure, but autumn meant football to me from the time I
could be pushed in my buggy or carried to the games.
And after-game parties with flaming chafing dishes, hot
chocolate or spiced cider, popcorn and apples were often
held at our home. My parents were young, closer to the
age of the students than most of their colleagues, and

comfortably popular. It was my good fortune to be part of their family, and when the students at this small Kansas college where my father taught psychology wished to honor him, they made a decision that now seems inconceivable—I was chosen Queen of the homecoming festivities. The young son of another favorite professor was dubbed King. Our royal photograph taken during the parade shows two happy and slightly bewildered children sitting on a decorated float drawn by college students in boaters and heavy sweaters. The girls wore shirtwaists and elegantly tailored skirts. They all carried thin bamboo canes with pennants to wave as they cheered. My father rode in this parade on a white horse. What he was supposed to represent, I have no idea, but another picture shows him in an ersatz coat of mail complete with helmet. He was no horseman, but his familiar smile wins out over a look of faint surprise.

Sadly enough, I hardly lived up to my glamorous beginnings. In college I was demoted to Princess, one of four members of the court. Perhaps I peaked too soon.

## Mother

In the mosaic of pictures of my mother that hangs in my bedroom is my favorite—the portrait of a beautiful dark-haired young woman in her wedding dress. It was taken in 1907 in Emporia, Kansas. Against the creamy white lace of the yoke hangs a gold cross on a heavy double-linked chain. A slender coral rosebud, like a tear, centers the cross. Mother loved the necklace, wore it frequently, and often made her decision about which dress to buy or have made based on which would look best with this favorite piece of jewelry. It is now mine, having miraculously escaped three separate burglaries, but I never wear it without feeling as though I were "dressing-up" in my mother's clothes.

Her wedding dress of lace and mull, exquisitely tucked and ruffled, lies in a cedar chest waiting to be worn again. It is now a deep rich cream and soft as spider webs to the touch.

My mother, sitting in a high-backed chair rising in an arch above her shoulders, looks as though she had found exactly what she wanted for the rest of her life— my father.

They had been childhood sweethearts from the time the dark-eyed little girl had moved from Gilfillan, Kansas near Fort Scott, to Moran, where Ralph Jewell, two years older, lived with his father, the town doctor, and his mother, who had been Mary Rebecca Coe. In a one-room schoolhouse, both had been good students, and the two-year grade gap made little difference. Mother went on to win medals in mathematics; my father was valedictorian, gifted in writing and speaking.

After high school, the long separations began. They each went to Highland Academy but two years apart, and by the time Mother was ready to enter, Daddy had left to attend Coe College in Cedar Rapids, Iowa. From there he went east for graduate study at Clark University in Worcester, Massachusetts. Mother spent only one year at Highland and then transferred to College of Emporia. They saw each other rarely on infrequent vacations, and their letters from that period fairly ache with longing, although Mother made the most of retelling her social life in a vein that would feed any bit of jealousy and yearning my father might feel! When I first found those letters in the storeroom below my Dickson Street playhouse, only Mother's uniquely flowing script identified them to me. The teasing tone, the gaiety and archness covering a passionate undercurrent of longing was the voice of a young woman I could barely recognize.

That she loved my father, totally, as he loved her, was a fact of my life and unquestioned. That she loved me I felt in the touch of her hands as she brushed my hair and smoothed it around her finger, as she put a cool, damp washcloth over my forehead on the rare occasions when I was sick, in the circle of her arms when I kissed her goodnight. We were a "touching" family, and to kiss or hug or pat or stroke was as familiar as breathing. Mother and Daddy made no show of their emotions, but her caress when she said, "Ralph, dear," or occasionally, "Jimmins," was revealing, indeed. My brother and I had no doubt as to the fact that they came first with each other. After all, they had created the family—we were the inevitable consequences! Such recognition gave us a powerful sense of security. They were the responsible ones in the area of family destiny. We had only to keep our rooms clean, brush our teeth, take our baths, eat what was served us on our plates at the table, be polite, avoid fighting when possible, and ask to be excused rather than bolting from the table. It never occurred to us that they wouldn't keep the family going without our help.

She felt keenly having had to leave college without a baccalaureate degree. Perhaps some heedless or unkind remark had cut her and wounded the pride she held high throughout her life. Mother knew how admired and respected she was by my father, but she wished to present impeccable academic credentials to anyone who might ask. As soon as we children were older, she began to take summer session courses at the university in literature, psychology, and art appreciation. This return to classes was unusual at the time, but no teacher ever had a more industrious student. Her eagerness and curiosity led her into research beyond that of the ordinary pupil. Stacks of books stood around her desk, all tagged with neat, torn paper bookmarks. File boxes of 3 X 5 cards jostled with each other for a favored place near the writing blotter. Looseleaf binders filled and took their places on nearby bookshelves. She was a meticulous and well-ordered note taker. Outlines came naturally to her logical mind.

The papers she turned in for course credit range from, "Thomas Hardy: A Romantic?" to "Oriental Art in Occidental Culture." She was often on the program of one of her clubs, presenting one of these papers or a sea-soned and sensitive book review. She and my father, both avid readers, had distinctly different tastes. My father had the more catholic taste, and on the low table by his big reading chair, a romance by Jeffrey Farnol or Ian MacLaren lay side by side with a psychology text and a Stephen Leacock or Robert Benchley. Mother's table probably held a book on *Early American Glass* by Ruth Webb Lee, *Oriental Art*, and a *Ladies Home Journal*. Their ongoing discussions led Jimmie and me to the in-formed opinion that agreement was not necessary in this world. Thoughtful and well-presented variants were far more interesting.

We especially loved to hear them embark on tales of Moran-town as seen by them in their childhood. Going to the same tiny school, living diagonally across the street from one another, junior citizens of a community of less than six hundred souls, they saw life so variously that each interrupted the other's stories to set the record straight and correct all of the details. "Ralph, it couldn't possibly have been Floy McGlashan. She was far too thin," or, "Edna, dear, Clare Kinne was a little older than I, not younger." With what different eyes they had seen the same small town—we egged them on to tell us more.

Mother's determination carried her to campuses in Arkansas, Oregon, and Texas. She finally received her cherished diploma from Trinity University in San Antonio after she was seventy. My father had gone there after his retirement in Oregon to help set up a new graduate school. How proud he was when his wife went on to take her master's degree in fine arts from that very school! Her work in design was outstanding, and she combined her theory courses with amazing creativity in painting, ceramics, and weaving, presenting a one-woman show in innovative methods and materials for weaving at the San Antonio museum. Her obvious pleasure in her art work made us very happy—we had known only that her home, her flower arrangements, and her eye for color were evidence of an active love of beauty. How exciting to see this unknown artist emerge! Her ceramics, clean lined and often heavy, especially have the look of being done by someone much younger, perhaps a man. Nothing irritated her more than to have some well-intentioned admirer say, "Mrs. Jewell, you're a regular Grandma Moses!"

As I remember, there were certain hours for many things as I was growing up—the most sacred of which was NAPTIME. My mother took a nap immediately after lunch almost every day of her life—every day if she were at home. If she went out to a luncheon, the nap was postponed until late afternoon when she had returned home. As a baby, I suppose, I had napped at the same time, but my taste for sleeping in the daytime disappeared early. Mother urged that I take books, as many as I wished, or a favorite doll to bed with me. I could look at pictures, read, play Mother as I chose, but I must remain in my bed, be perfectly quiet. Finally, I was allowed to be up and around in other parts of the house, still noiseless except for my new responsibility—answering the phone. Instructions were to lift the receiver, say,

"Dr. Jewell's residence," and then follow questions about my mother with, "I'm sorry, she's resting. May I have your name so that she may call you back, or may I take the message?" This first lesson in social dependability has, sadly enough, resulted in my continuing belief that the telephone is a necessary evil, to be used only for the briefest, most urgent communication.

Mother's inviolate naptimes with her door tightly closed against all comers must have been a necessary bulwark to her need for privacy. Never have I known anyone with such an intense regard for her inner self. Although she was interested in people, fond of her friends, and almost jealous of her family, people exhausted her. After celebrations of any kind, she spent days recovering from her fatigue. She had to be alone, and only my father could breach that tightly closed door. He would tap quietly on the door, push it open, and then we would hear his low gentle voice talking to her: "Edna, dear—." Sometimes he would be able to bring her out with him, but more often he would say to us, "We'll have dinner without your mother tonight. Elizabeth will fix her some tea." I am sure that Daddy's background as a psychologist helped him understand and support her desperate need at such times to withdraw—even from him.

Mother could be irritated, too, by laziness, untidiness of person, pompousness of any kind. She did not "suffer fools gladly" but she was compassionate, curious, and a great celebrator of whatever came to hand to celebrate. All holidays were honored with special decorations and menus. Her effort to bring me into the mood of Hallowe'en had been a near disaster. Everything else was a success. Valentine's Day was full of hearts and flowers, lace paper valentines, molded salads quivering heart-shaped at each place, little frilled cups filled with conversation candies that asked or commanded, "Be my Valentine," "Do you love me?," "Say when!"

St. Patrick's Day was awash with shamrocks and tiny clay pipes. We were sent off to school in clothes as green as grass—no one ever had occasion to give us a pinch because we'd forgotten the bright apparel. Although no one liked corned beef very much, we had it with cabbage for St. Patrick's Day dinner every year— and the salads were green.

Perhaps Easter was her favorite, and she made a fine blend of the secular and the religious in her observance. We hunted Easter eggs that might have been designed by Faberge, had he been more limited in his materials, inside or out according to the weather. Rabbits, chicks, and ducklings abounded. My favorite Jordan almonds filled nests of cut green paper—the best eggs I could imagine. And there was always my carefully chosen new Easter dress and hat or bonnet (one year a huge sailor with broad streamers, one year a Milan straw bonnet with field flowers). The dress became my "best dress" for the year; last year's costume, if I hadn't grown out of it yet, served as second best.

Thanksgiving was always a very special family day, celebrated at church and at home with more food than one could possibly eat, bowls and baskets of fruits and vegetables spilling over onto the table, and what seemed to me an overlong prayer of gratitude for all that we enjoyed. (If God knew everything, I figured, surely he knew how happy we all were!)

And when Christmas time was close upon us, Mother fairly glowed with holiday spirit and gave herself over completely to preparations for the great day.

Mother and Daddy shaped a tradition that scarcely varied from year to year: hanging stockings on Christmas Eve with a reading of the First Christmas, a cup of hot cocoa and a cookie and off to bed after fixing a

glass of milk and a cookie for Santa, the lighting of carefully sheltered candles in the windows to show the
Christ Child's weary parents that there was room for
them with us.

Christmas morning brought stockings often stuffed
with more than they could hold. Small packages that
wouldn't fit were piled below. Always along with ribbon
candy and those wonderful cut sticks centered with tiny
pine trees or canes or stars, we found a new washcloth,
toothpaste and brush, and a bar of each one's favorite
soap. An orange was stuffed in the toe, the washcloth
usually came next, and an apple rounded the heel.
Brazil nuts, pecans and almonds fitted in around bar-
rettes, a folded new hair ribbon wrapped in protective
tissue paper, jacks and a ball, and, buried deep, a special treasure—perhaps a ring or bracelet.

Christmas dinner was an anti-climax even though
the table shone in white damask, gleaming silver, bubbles of crystal. Red candles flickered over the holly and
ivy. It was a formal dinner and Mother used her most
treasured china, a feathered gold and white Haviland.
We seldom had guests. The four of us—five when Baby
Keith was with us for three short years—were captured
in a bubble of Christmas joy.

Smaller bubbles held the delight of each birthday.
Mother once built a log cabin of candy sticks for my
brother, who celebrated a February date, as had
Abraham Lincoln. One year she baked three birthday
cakes in sad succession for my father—inexplicably,
they kept falling. I saw the silent tears stream down her
cheeks as she frosted the last one. She made and sent
four-layer birthday cakes to us long after we had left
home for school or work. Somehow she exerted a special
spell over the United States Postal Service, because these
treats usually arrived in great shape, barely crumpled
from their journey.

She collected china, her special Haviland and also Limoges and English earthenware; early American pressed glass, especially tiny individual and family salt dishes (over four hundred stood in corner cabinets built especially for them in the dining room), Oriental art objects—prints, fabrics, small vases—as well as stamps and coins. My father became a ready supplier of "corners" for her stamp collection and haunted the post office windows to bring her fresh sheets of new issues. They plotted together to send self-addressed envelopes away to various addresses in order to have them returned, the cover bearing a First Day cancellation. When my son started a coin collection, he and Mother excitedly discussed their acquisitions, evaluating and formally trading extra coins. She never let him raid her store and, indeed, never showed him her total collection. For Mother, what was hers was *hers*.

We had many a difficult time as I was growing up because our temperaments were so very different, but I always felt cherished and knew that I was. Perhaps that very fact gave me something to rebel against. Then, too, Mother was almost always right and that infuriated me. If she suggested a method of doing something, from cleaning my room to solving an algebra problem, it turned out to be the best way. And if one failed to perform it satisfactorily, Mother said quietly, "I am sure you wouldn't be satisfied to leave it at that." She took care of a careless brick mason once in just that manner when she pointed out a slight misalignment in the fireplace he had almost completed. To his surprise, but not to my mother's, the offending firebox was torn out and relaid. Both were satisfied with the result!

I have said my mother was almost always right. I would have said "always" and left it at that, but such an unqualified statement is hard for those who didn't know her to believe. Not that she was overbearing or flaunted her correctness but that somehow she really knew best. Domestic helpers, burdened at first with her precise instructions, came to depend on her wisdom and ended as devoted friends because of her kindness and consistent fairness. They soon learned that in the kitchen there were always two sets of tea towels to be used—the white ones, made of bleached flour sacks whose chain-stitched seams I loved to pull, were for china and silver; the blue ones, whose origin I never knew or have forgotten, were for pots and pans. They were not interchangeable and no goblet was ever smeared with a greasy towel! The tea towels were sent to the laundry weekly with the sheets and towels and shirts and hung on their kitchen racks in starchy order.

## The Green-Eyed Monster

Picture a happy family of three: father, a handsome young professional man, talented, understanding, in love with people and beloved by them; mother, beautiful, devoted, quick-minded, curious; four-year-old daughter, healthy, bright, sure of her position in the triad. What need had they of a baby son, brother, rival?

The puzzle repeated itself over and over in my mind as I tried to understand and cope with what had happened to me, to us. It had been shock enough to waken one morning and be told by an excited and obviously delighted father that the fictional baby was here; to be taken into their bedroom, where I saw my mother propped up on pillows, a bit pale and exhausted but looking every bit as happy as my father; to find a strange woman in starchy white bringing to my mother a small red object swaddled in flannels. But to find that the baby stayed on long after the excitement had passed and drew from my parents the same loving care they had lavished on me was a continuing trauma. Somehow I must have failed them, left undone what I ought to have done, unwittingly done what I should never have done. Otherwise, my mind told me, they wouldn't have needed this interloper. For some reason, I couldn't talk about it with them, although I was normally an extremely articulate and confiding child. They seemed so sublimely pleased with the situation.

Worse still, Jimmie grew into a picture-book baby. Blond, petite, eyes round and blue, cheeks so pink that strangers would stop my mother as she wheeled the carriage on our daily walks to exclaim over "those darling apple cheeks." He was interested in the world around him and played serenely with whatever came to hand.

# *Two*

# First Home in the Ozarks

## *Moving South*

OUR NEW family of four left Emporia in the late summer of 1913 to move south into the Ozarks. Daddy had accepted a position on the faculty of the University of Arkansas where he was to be dean of the newly created College of Education. The opportunity to work toward his dreams of what schools could and should be intrigued him. He was not dismayed by the state's lowly position among its peers, fortieth or so, in the realm of public education. We faced more changes than we knew.

I remember very little of our travel to Fayetteville except for one vivid picture of the four of us in the dark of a small railway station waiting for a train to which we would transfer to continue our journey. Mother sat on a low baggage trolley holding Jimmie in her arms; six months old, he slept soundly. What little light there was from a crossing signal painted a chiaroscuro portrait of Mother's white face, dark hair blowing a bit under her big traveling hat. She didn't look quite like my mother.

But I held tightly to Daddy's hand, fingers engulfed in his warm grasp. We walked a short way down the tracks where our suitcases and steamer trunks were heaped in a casual pile. Daddy's eyeglasses caught the meager light with a reassuring gleam as we returned to

31

stand by Mother and the baby. It was fitting that we should stay together on this great adventure—one that kept us so far from home in the middle of the night when surely we should be safely in bed.

I can't remember the arrival of the train for which we waited or anything about climbing aboard. Perhaps my four-year-old body had insisted on its own rights and fallen asleep. It may have been easier for my parents, thirty-five and thirty-three, to cope with the transfer and direct the reloading of the baggage to have both children sound asleep—no questions to answer, no demands for food or drink—as they went on their way into the new life that lay ahead.

Arriving safely, we made our way to our new home on Leverett Street, number 538, low, white, surrounded by a wide veranda that held a deep porch swing. Behind it sprawled a rusty red barn with a sloping roof that touched the fence. Later on, I was able to make this roof my own—much to my mother's dismay. The lawn held the customary elms, maples, and catalpa trees, rose bushes and a round bed for annuals, usually nasturtiums, that I used to try to jump over in one of my fits of athletic prowess. I tripped and fell into it on one of these leaps, cutting my knee deeply on unseen pieces of broken glass. My first tetanus shot followed, administered by Dr. Ellis, who had become our trusted family doctor.

Our house stood across the street from a tall yellow Victorian, very stylish, I thought, with its high steps to the front door. To the left of our house toward the campus, which was only a block away, lived Mrs. Richardson, a widow, and her two sons, Fount (short for Fontaine) and Bat (nickname in place of Davis). They were big boys, in high school, and to my admiring eyes as handsome as the proverbial Greek gods. They were also very nice to me—gave me boosts up the maple "climbing tree" until I was tall enough to reach the critical bottom branch myself and swung me around and around by my arms in big swooping circles.

Their attitude was in great contrast to Arthur Harding's. The elder brother of Mary Frances, who lived in the yellow Victorian, was said to be the smartest boy in town. He fully agreed with that estimate. His father, later head of the mathematics department at the university and later still its president, wore pince-nez— a feat of skill and daring that I greatly admired. He was a rather formal man, not one to encourage intimacy with children. Mrs. Harding was rather formal, too, always fastidiously dressed and with a well-deserved reputation as an extraordinary hostess.

Mary Frances became my closest friend and most contentious rival. She was only a few months older than I and we competed for grades, friends, and overall achievement. Mary Frances had some natural advantages that I reluctantly acknowledged—she was prettier than I, more petite and blessed with musical talent. More important as we grew up was her innate social skill, carefully groomed by her mother, and her earlier sexual development and appeal. Mary Frances was simply more worldly than I—and successfully so. I recognized and grieved over this.

The block to the campus, downhill all the way, was soon my path to school where a small experimental enterprise was convened in Peabody Hall, the new education building. My first day there was marked by an incident at recess that showed what a different world we had entered with our move to Arkansas. A new friend invited me to share the teeter-totter with her, and as we rose and fell with the board she asked, "Where did you all come from?"

Eagerly, I shared the information, "Kansas— Emporia, Kansas!" It gave me a feeling of happy identity to call out the name of my former home.

Betty jumped off her end of the board as it came down. "I can't play with you," she yelled. "My grandfather made me promise never to play with any Damn Yankee! Go back to Kansas. I won't ever play with you."

My end of the board hit the ground with a jolt that ran up my spine and threatened to knock off my head. Betty had flounced off toward the flying rings, surrounded by an admiring group of friends. I stood alone, nauseous from the fall I had taken, confusedly wondering what a Damn Yankee could possibly be. How did I get to be one?

I abandoned school, ran off the playground and down the campus steps toward home and my mother. She was startled by my untimely appearance—disheveled and panting from my run, tears making their way down flushed cheeks. "Honey girl?" she asked as she opened her arms to me.

Sobbing now, I blurted out my painful story. Mother's face paled as I implored, "What's a Damn Yankee, Mama? What's a Damn Yankee?"

Her greatly loved father, who died in my infancy, had fought in the Union Army during the Civil War. I had looked many times at his little wooden hand trunk, shaped like a log, covered with shiny deerskin, the hair preserved only around the nailheads that formed his initials, CBK. The cask, I knew, held letters from that period, some written by him, some written by his nurses in the field hospital where he lay for months after being wounded. Mother had never said more to me than, "Handle it carefully, dear. The Civil War was very long ago."

Now Mother reached for her silver-backed mirror on the dresser. She held it in front of my swollen face. "See, dear—it is you. The ugly words can't change you. Betty's a child, just like you. Her grandfather spoke in anger. Soon you and Betty will be friends again." I wasn't too sure about that, but Mother called Peabody to explain that I was not feeling well and would not be back that afternoon. Then she held me and explained that when people were angry enough to fight, they were also angry enough to call each other names.

(She was right about Betty. Our friendship has survived some rocky times but is treasured and alive today.)

## My Mother the Ghost

Celebrations were my mother's delight. She made an occasion of every special day, decorating the house in red, white, and blue or Easter pastels and painted eggs, choosing appropriate menus, making or selecting favors for each of us and whatever guests we had. And so she wanted me to love all this as she did, and my father later told me they had talked at length about how to prevent terror from entering into Hallowe'en. "She mustn't be frightened," Mother said. "I'll be a ghost and take off my hood and show her who I am and that it's fun to make-believe."

Dark came early on Hallowe'en night. The three of us sat down to dinner, the table holding a jack-o'-lantern like the one at the front door. The pumpkin faces were wreathed in enormous smiles and had one snaggle tooth apiece with round candlelit eyes. I had helped carve them. It was our first holiday celebration since we had moved from Kansas to the Ozarks, and with my baby brother already asleep, I felt very much part of my parents' adult world. I was just five. Candles flickered over the black cats, witches, and small white ghosts surrounding the pumpkin centerpiece. It was warm and happy to be just the three of us again.

Although our dessert, an orange sherbet and chocolate cookies, had been served, Mother looked across at my father and asked if she might be excused. This was unusual because it was a rule that one stay at the table until everyone was through. But Daddy nodded and asked me if I thought I'd like another cookie. Several minutes passed; Mother did not return and then the doorbell rang.

Daddy popped up from his chair, shook his head at the hired girl whose face appeared at the kitchen door and held out his hand to me. "Come with me," he invited. "We'll see who's out on Hallowe'en." I was never permitted to answer the door at night and literally jumped off my chair at the chance offered me. We went into the wide hall and toward the heavy front door.

The porch light was on as usual and bathed in its glow was an apparition, a ghost all in white, saying in a cracked voice, "Trick or treat, little girl, trick or treat!" I jerked my hand from my father's, turned and ran screaming back down the hall to the safety of the dining room. Plunging under the long tablecloth, I clung to the big oak pedestal and sobbed and sobbed and sobbed. They came after me, calling endearments and consolation and apology. My mother's fine dark hair was all askew from her pillowcase hood, pulled hastily, carelessly, off and thrown aside. "Honey girl, honey girl," she murmured as she held me. "There, there—it's Mother. We didn't mean to frighten you."

The three of us clutched each other beside the pedestal under the table. Who was most frightened would be hard to say.

## To Grandfather's House

All the way on the hot train ride, my heart pounding with the hazard of changing trains in Muskogee, I could see the orchard, cool and leafy beside the austere New England house, miraculously transplanted to a tiny Kansas town. As I itched from the wiry green plush and my eyes stung with cinders, the picture sustained me. Two-storied, a deep mustard color, windows like sentry boxes, restrained wooden embroidery along the eaves, the house presented a black iron knocker under the nameplate, James E. Jewell, M.D.

We were never met at the station but made our way like pilgrims up the brick path with its rickrack edging. Marvelously, the door flew open before we could sound the knocker. My slender, enduring grandmother embraced her son, my father. Murmuring, "Ralph, oh, Ralph," she let tears roll unheeded down her cheeks. Uncle Doctor, my grandfather, stood a bit aside, pride in his son and dignity in his role as patriarch fighting a fierce battle behind the erect posture, elegantly trimmed beard, and eloquent eyes, until they could clasp hands and elbows, stating firmly, "Father!," "Son!" Watching the divinely dictated ceremony of greeting, my brother and I made an impatient unit around Mother, properly waiting our turn. No one was forgotten. Mother had been almost a part of the household since childhood and was tenderly welcomed.

At last we could move out of the severe and formal entry, with its beveled glass mirror and its folding rack for hats, into the special fragrance of the parlor. Lace curtains clouded the purpose of the sentry windows, cord-bound draperies framed the tempered light. The wallpaper resolved itself into stripes mounting higher and higher toward a ceiling, too remote for my awestruck eyes. Books were everywhere, standing on parade in the glass-fronted cases, lying at stylish angles on polished tables. They were read, I knew, for they were talked about, questioned, challenged at the dinner table and afterwards in the orchard. But for me the parlor had one purpose only—to enthrone the organ waiting there across from the windows for my skinny legs to pump it into life. It was accustomed to hymns and demanded strenuous effort to bring it to 6/8 time. "Apple Blossoms," which after considerable practice rippled on our piano, had a "More Stately Mansions" tone on the organ. The grown-ups heard me once through, praised me, kissed me, and went back to their own country—talking, talking, talking.

Stealing into the dining room, its long table set for dinner, I took a gingersnap from the ironstone tureen in the corner cupboard, popped it into my mouth, and filched a handful for my pocket. Then I counted the plates to see how many for dinner—just family, I hoped—and lost myself in spicy smells from the kitchen.

Should I go up the narrow enclosed stairway to find my featherbed in the Blue Room with its angled ceiling or tiptoe into the majesty of my grandparents' bedroom? Rare was the chance to slip alone into the Big Bedroom. As the door opened, my eyes filled with the enormous bed, dark headboard rising to the ceiling, blue and white coverlet from the Tennessee mountains reaching to the floor and hiding the trundlebed. Sometimes one was fortunate enough to fall ill and be returned to health in this rolled out haven.

The most important part of this room in my eyes was the narrow door to Grandmother's prayer closet, tucked away in the angle under the stairs. The awesome determination with which she entered to speak with God, "have at" this world's pain and injustice, and settle such problems as were emergent made her re-entry into the busy rounds of doctor's wife and community confidante all the more impressive. Once she and God had made a decision, mere man was pushed aside. She was not without fun, however. Her gaiety and wit were legendary, and it was she who once dyed the family cat in her son's class colors!

At last the call came for midday dinner, notable as always for the glowing grapes at Uncle Doctor's place (applesauce for us). Formal grace began the meal, then a rapid roll call of friends and relatives, their current conditions, physical and spiritual, and a careful prognosis for each. Food was briefly honored in the eating and by quiet compliments. For me, eager to run outside into the orchard, it took a very long time.

My grandfather pushed back his chair, rose, said to my grandmother, "May, we will meet you in the orchard," and took my hand. First, we would go to his office, out the front door and down the side path to a miniature of the New England house. Unlocking the door with a heavy key, he led me into the parlor-like waiting room, through his office and into the examining room, where a mysteriously high table stood beside a reclining chair. Instruments lay in folded white towels, diagrams of the eye stared from the wall. In the corner a tall, forbidding pharmaceutical cabinet rose to the ceiling. Behind its glass doors stood bottles and flasks with labels I could not read, although Ipecac, Laudanum, carbolic acid, and quinine were familiar. On a convenient shelf, powders and papers were ready.

My breath caught. From an opened drawer Grandfather took a box of empty capsules, counted twelve into my hand, cautioned me as a fellow professional that my dolls would recover from any illness if these medicines were carefully dispensed. We nodded formally to each other in complete understanding and went out to join the others.

In the angle behind the office and beside the house stood the cherry orchard. Eight or nine trees, ankle-deep in grass, made a canopy of leaves over the lawn chairs and Uncle Doctor's reclining throne. On one side was the grape arbor, each perfect bunch carefully tied in a peppermint-striped confectioner's bag to foil marauding birds or insects. The orchard was a place for dreams. Lying on the grass, breathing the warm earth, drowsy eyes blurring the reds and yellows and oranges of the portulacca spilling out of a dull blue enamel bowl set into the stump of the one cherry tree that had dared to die, mesmerized by the flow of grown-up talk, I fell asleep— capsules safe in hand.

## Far From the Catskills

My father, James Ralph Jewell, was born on March 2, 1878, in Athens, Tennessee, in the heart of the Smokies. He had been the second son of James Erastus Jewell and Mary Rebecca Coe. Married in February, 1868, they had gone to Talledega, Alabama, where together with Professor Luke, a Canadian, they founded Talledega College for "Freedmen, the newly emancipated colored people." The college was maintained under the auspices of the American Board of Commissioners for Foreign Missions of the Congregational Church. It was also partially supported by the federal Freedmen's Bureau.

Grandma's father, Daniel Coe, a long time supporter of emancipation, had made his home in New York State one of the stations on the Underground Railway before and during the Civil War. He moved to Talledega after the war and bought timber tracts and sawmills. In that way, he hoped to be able to provide employment for the former slaves and also for the many poor whites, a comparatively new segment of the population.

On March 15, 1870, Frank Andrus Jewell was born to the young couple. He lived for only two months. In October, Grandma's best Alabama friend died in childbirth. The baby, Walter, was taken to my grandparents' home, named Walter Coe Jewell, and brought up as their son. His own father and family moved to Utah. Later that disastrous year, Daniel Coe's lumberyard and mills were burned by the Ku Klux Klan. Professor Luke, who with his wife had lived in a double house with Grandma and Grandpa and her father, was hanged from a tree in front of that house. The charge was, "They taught niggers!"

The lynchers of Professor Luke were understandably wary of closing in on my grandfather, who had a well-deserved reputation as an unusually accurate shot. In consequence, he managed to escape on foot into the "knobs" of East Tennessee, where there were few Confederate sympathizers.

My grandmother had severely injured her back in attempts to fight the flames. She and baby Walter and her father remained in Alabama, where she was confined to bed for some time. And then her father died—the exact date and circumstances remain unclear. Apparently more than a year elapsed before my grandparents could be reunited in Tennessee, where Grandpa had established a tannery. His youngest brother, Anson, joined him, coming south from the family home in the Catskills. They operated the yard in partnership.

Grandpa, who had "read medicine" in the office of his father, James Jewell, M.D., in Catskill, New York, and helped him unofficially in his practice, was increasingly asked by the mountain people for medical help. In 1876, he decided, after earnest correspondence with his father, to go to Baltimore and enroll in the regular medical course of the College of Physicians and Surgeons. The year following his graduation, the college became Johns Hopkins University. He was the gold medal-winning graduate, and his ornate diploma now hangs on the living room wall in my brother's home.

Grandpa's attendance at medical school was from 1879 to 1881, so he missed seeing my father grow from infancy into early childhood. What my grandmother's life was like with her husband away in Baltimore and her two sons, Walter, ten, and Ralph, almost two, is perhaps best left to the imagination.

In March of 1881, my grandfather returned from Baltimore and rejoined his family. My grandfather was not a mountain man, and by the following year he and Anson, not yet married, decided that they could not in good conscience bring up children in such a limited environment. And so in the late summer of 1882, James Erastus Jewell, M.D., and his brother Anson "left East Tennessee, driving northward and westward in a light spring wagon, looking for a suitable location for a new home where there would be prospects of good schools and good community influences for their children." They crossed the Mississippi at Cap Girardeau, spent a day or so in Rolla, Missouri and, going steadily westward, passed through Fort Scott and traveled on to Moran.

There they met Dr. Henry Strong, a former surgeon in the federal army during the Civil War. Dr. Strong wanted to retire; my grandfather hoped to buy a practice. After a few days exploration of the little town and countryside and a trip to Iola, ten miles away and the county seat, Grandpa and Anson decided to settle permanently in Moran. The practice Grandpa bought had a radius of one hundred miles!

## Mary Rebecca Coe

*My play here must be close;*
*I can't run free.*
*No one comes calling—*
*Play parties are for others.*

*The piney woods in the hot sun,*
*Pitch running in amber clots*
*Smells clean and harsh—*
*Not like the greenwood Catskills*
*Where I played in gentler summers.*
*The soft slow speech of those around me*
*Is kinder to the ear*
*Than the crisp old Yankee talk.*

*Drawls can turn ugly though,*
*And full of hate.*
*"Damn nigger lover!" is spat*
*With the venom of a copperhead*
*Toward my father,*
*Tall uncompromising Daniel Coe.*
*(He had made his Northern home*
*A station for black people*
*Running to freedom in Canada.)*

*For weeks The Mill has been forbidden*
*ground.*
*No longer may I feel*
*The hard sure hand of my father*
*Leading me safely past*
*The bright saw blades that*
*Slash through pungent timber*
*While I sniff the sawdust piles*
*Gold in the sun.*

*Something is happening here*
*That children mustn't know.*

*I wake from uneasy sleep*
*To the glare of unleashed flames,*
*The hiss of resin,*
*An explosion of sparks*
*Against the black night.*

*My mother, shawl over nightdress,*
*Wraps me in a wet quilt.*
*We run from the house.*

*Like a monstrous bonfire,*
*The Mill is burning.*

*A circle of men in white, with torches,*
*Throw other torches into the blaze.*
*Jumping, running, yelling,*
*Drunk on their own excitement,*
*They fail to see us*
*As we join a haggard figure—*
*My father, black with soot,*

*To hide in the bushes*
*Far from the Catskills.*

## Cyclone Summer

It must have been the summer I was seven-going-on-eight that the mantle of responsibility fell so heavily over my shoulders that I was all but engulfed in it. My father, who had been increasingly disabled by acute abdominal pain, was told by Dr. Ellis, our dear friend and medical oracle, that he must go to the Mayo Clinic for extensive surgery too sophisticated for the Fayetteville hospital, where he had been taken. Mother was to go with him and live near the clinic until he was able to make the trip home. My brother Jimmie, who was three, and I were to travel to Kansas with a cousin of Mother's, Aunt Emma to us, and live in her home for the duration.

Our own home had seemed very strange ever since Daddy became ill. To see him consumed by pain was frightening, and to miss his usual teasing and loving humor made me lonely. It was hard to understand and nothing was the same. When Mother sat with her arm around me and told me the plans, her voice broke and her eyes were bright with unshed tears. She emphasized that each one of us must do whatever we could to help Daddy get well again. I could tell that she was frightened, too.

"You are older than Jimmie," she pointed out, "and Daddy and I are very fortunate that you will be able to help Aunt Emma and Grandma and Grandpa take care of him. I don't know what we would do without you. You'll be a good girl, I know." She gave me a tight squeeze and some of her tears spilled out.

The very next day Aunt Emma arrived, rosy-cheeked and bustling. She busied herself packing our suitcases and straightening up the house before everyone's departure. I was awed to learn that my handsome father was to be taken to the train from the hospital in his pajamas. A bed would be ready for him in the Pullman car. Mother packed a suit, some shirts, and other clothes for him "to come home in." I couldn't believe any part of this—Daddy was always the one who carried the tickets, saw that the luggage was aboard, and tipped the porter.

He loved to travel and made jokes all the while. Now he was being taken away on one train while we waited for another.

Later that day, Aunt Emma, Jimmie, and I were taken back down to the old Katy station by a friend and soon were chugging off to Muskogee on the way to Kansas. The green plush seats scratched when I sat down, and the smell of cinders and smoke nudged my anxiety into early symptoms of "train sickness." Everyone in my family, including my small brother, knew that "Margaret gets car sick"—and train sick and trolley-car sick and sea sick. Aunt Emma, however, had not been primed with this information, and when I asked to go to the restroom at the end of the car, she patted me on the shoulder and said, "Not now, dear. We haven't been on our way long enough for the conductor to take the tickets. Just sit like a good girl and look out the window."

Looking out the window was not what I needed, but I tried to sit still. Jimmie was happily licking a big lollipop, given him at the station. I tried not to look at him and not to smell the sweet, fruity candy. Waves of nausea rolled over me. The muscles of my jaw clenched tight. I pushed up to stand, but Aunt Emma pulled me down beside her. "Would you like a drink of water?" she asked.

That did it. Desperately I lunged out of my seat and into the aisle, headed for the restroom. I didn't make it. Choking and gagging, I was immediately and violently ill. Realizing too late that my request for privacy was valid, my aunt half carried me, half supported me down the aisle to the highly varnished door with its brass plate: LADIES. It was a long time before the wet towels and ice brought by the porter calmed my convulsive vomiting. I was covered with shame, glad only that my trusting mother did not know how quickly her "good girl" had betrayed her trust.

When we reached Moran, the very small town in southeast Kansas where my parents had grown up and where my father's parents still lived, I had determined to make up for my miserable performance en route by living an exemplary life throughout the summer and by seeing to it that my brother followed my glowing example. This was easier dreamed than done. Jimmie was an active, bright, almost dramatically handsome child. Strangers on the street often assured him that he had "cheeks like apples" and asked him where he got them. It was hard not to let my green-eyed envy show when this happened, and my mother often eased it by lifting one of my dark curls or putting an arm around my shoulders. Now she was far away, wherever Minnesota was, and Jimmie was my responsibility.

Naturally curious, he easily upset Aunt Emma's daily schedule. Her children were Veva, just finishing high school, and Wanda, newly married and setting up her own home. Neither had ever been a mischievous little boy.

Finally my brother was naughty enough in some way I can't remember to be banished from a summer evening supper out under the peach trees in the side yard. His bed was rolled under the open window so that he could watch the party and be somewhat supervised. Enchanted with this, he held court as relatives and neighbors came by to greet him. He couldn't have had a better time. I was embarrassed for him. A sullen advocate of truly punitive discipline, I felt that he should somehow be made to feel and act guilty and morose.

His ability to make the best and most creative use of circumstances beyond his control flowered when we were taken to the Methodist church for the first time. Brought up in the rather chilly Presbyterian faith, I was surprised and pleased by the unexpected rhythm and dancing tempos of the evangelical hymns. And sitting erect during the long sermon, I meditated on how proud I would make the family of my deportment in this strange church. Then I noticed that people were turning toward our family group, smiling and prodding others, who also turned and smiled. Jimmie, two seats away from me, was the focus of their attention. Sublimely unconscious of being watched, he leaned forward to take a small collection envelope from the metal filigree pocket on the back of the pew ahead, opened it carefully, spat into it with admirable accuracy, and sealed it with a careful lick of his pink tongue. Would God strike him dead on the spot for such desecration? I rather hoped so! Tugging at the sleeve of Uncle Harry's jacket (he sat between us), I pointed out what was happening and was amazed at the chuckle that escaped him as he put an end to my brother's peaceful occupation. My pride in good behavior had suffered an irreparable blow. The story of Ralph and Edna's son's ingenuity was told over and over in Moran throughout the summer. Opinion had it that he was a caution!

Fearful for my father, whose dangerous condition had been complicated by peritonitis—a word foreign to me but always accompanied by head shaking and sad faces—I escaped from my responsibilities at Aunt Emma's whenever possible to visit Grandma and Grandpa, my father's parents. Grandpa, had retired as a physician, and was a semi-invalid who still treated me with grave dignity. Grandma, as near a saint as I will ever know, was so like my father in her lively sense of humor and love of life that she eased my loneliness as soon as I was with her. They, too, were frantic with worry about Daddy, but Grandpa showed me pictures of the abdominal cavity, pointed out the stomach and gall bladder, discussed ulcers and stones as if with a colleague, and left me feeling that I somehow knew a little about what was going on. Grandma took me into her prayer closet off the big bedroom under the stairs and introduced me to her God, with whom she openly and worshipfully worked through every crisis, big or little, of her life. Often she would say, "We will have to ask God about that," and disappear into her closet. She would emerge, face serene and set about whatever she and Our Father had decided.

Midafternoon on one of my visits to them, I was urged to hurry back to Aunt Emma's before what looked like an approaching storm really blew up. I trudged off in anything but a hurry. The hot air hung heavy around me and, as I pushed through, felt full of menace. Suddenly its quiet weight burst into turbulence. Gusts shook the cottonwood trees; leaves and twigs blew from the branches; a shingle or two sliced through the sky. The light changed into the mustard yellow of a thunderstorm, but as I stared over my shoulder an enormous cloud pushed its gray face toward me. The wind was concentrated on my back, a force more powerful than I had ever imagined. I was blown into a stumbling run and then, to my awe, I became airborne. Picked up by an invisible hand, I was carried straight down the street. No one had to tell me that I was in a cyclone. I had not read and re-read *The Wizard of Oz* for nothing. Was the Kingdom of Oz to be mine? Would I meet the Scarecrow and the Tin Woodman and the Cowardly Lion? What of the Wizard himself? And, most important to me, would I see Ozma?

To my extreme disappointment, I was put down as gently as I had been lifted, almost before my wandering thoughts had formed. I was a couple of blocks down the street from where my airlift had begun. I didn't hurry home, hoping that the magic carpet would come again, but eventually I found myself at Aunt Emma's, surprised by her tearful welcome. She and my grandparents had called back and forth on their wall-hung windup telephones, each hoping that I would be found safe at the other's home. I was pleasurably regarded as somewhat of a miracle to have survived the storm. In a nearby part of town there had been serious damage: trees down, roofs off, a slab of corrugated metal sliced into the side of a house.

My heart was light—I had at least been good enough to save!

## The Artist

I never knew my grandparents on my mother's side of the family; Corwin Bateman Keith died when I was six months old, and his wife, many years younger had died when Mother was a young woman.

Mother's devotion to her family was part of her intense loyalty to those she loved. Her father's presence in her new home in Moran was welcome in every way. I did not know him because he died when I was six months old, but a tiny scar on my cheek is a legacy from the Masonic badge he always wore in his lapel. A faded yellow poster on my wall was published on December 25, 1894 by the merchants and professional men of Emporia. A large ad identifies C. B. Keith as a Grain Dealer who "Always Pays Top Prices for All Kinds of Grain, Flax, Millet, Ground Feed, Field and Garden Seeds. Also has for sale the Finest Hard and Soft Coal." His photograph is distinguished by the direct gaze he passed on to his daughter and the full, almost bushy moustache—very much his own.

Papa, as my mother always called him, was an important figure in her life. Papa had lost Ella, his first wife, and their baby, Mary Alice, in childbirth three years before he married my grandmother, Mary Josephine Gilfillan. She was twenty years younger than her thirty-six-year-old groom. Josephine was a superb rider and an artist, who must have found it difficult at times to give housekeeping and motherhood first place in her life. She tried in her own independent spunky way, but lost her first baby, a boy, Essie, before he was a year old and gave birth to my mother, Edna Lucena Keith, on January 12, 1880. My grandmother later that year, in November, celebrated her nineteenth birthday.

Her mothering must have been sporadic, and Papa filled in his daughter's need for what is now called "parenting." My mother's fierce loyalty to her mother led to almost total supression of verbal memories about her, although our home was filled with her enormous oil paintings in ornate gold frames. Two oils, one of hollyhocks and another of The Old Mill, still hang in my home. It was from my father that I was to hear of the tragedy of which my mother never spoke. Josephine Gilfillan Keith was either thrown from her horse or knocked off its back by a heavy tree limb she somehow failed to see. Found unconscious after the frantic horse pounded home riderless to his stable, she regained consciousness and lived but had suffered massive head injuries beyond the medical skill of the time. Her life ended in the Kansas State Hospital for the Insane. She was not yet forty. My mother was twenty-one.

And so it was of Papa that Mother always spoke. "Papa would like," "Papa preferred," or simply, "Papa said." He had served in the Civil War in his very young manhood as a soldier in the Grand Army of the Republic until injuries and illness forced him into a field hospital for many months. My brother has the small round wooden casque that protected Grandpa's letters telling of the pain and deprivation of war, the kindness of his nurses, his longing for home. How I wish that I might consciously remember his voice!

### Please Come

*Cor, someone said I fell from a horse.*
*What a crazy thing to say. I have never*
*Fallen from a horse in my life—*
*Jumps or races! But I will admit that*
*Colonel was a handful—even for me.*
*And with all his spirit, he could shy*
*At nothing and buck—like those*
*Broncos, cow ponies, we saw at the*
*Exposition in San Francisco.*
*Remember?*

*There is a crescent scar on my head*
*Where my hair was cut so short—but now*
*It hardly shows. That's where the headaches*
*Start and the lightning strikes and I see*
*All the glittering fireworks before the*
*Rockets turn toward me and I have to*
*Run and hide. I'm more frightened, though,*
*When it turns dark—black—smothering. How*
*Can you hide from the dark? They catch me*
*And hold me and force my mouth open to*
*Swallow those pills that make me sleep.*
*Sometimes I sleep for days, I guess.*

*Cor, where is our daughter? My locket*
*Is gone now but her face comes to me*
*In dreams. Her curls are like mine but*
*Her eyes are yours. Does she still*
*Walk home from school with that*
*Handsome boy, the doctor's son? Do you*
*Suppose—she'd need me then, though*
*I'm a better artist and rider than a mother.*
*You've said the same—to tease me.*

*Are you so far away that you can't*
*Come to see me? Have you ever come?*
*Sometimes I don't remember what I see*
*But often I see things that others can't.*
*If you would send my paints or even*
*Charcoal, I would make those pictures*
*Real. Then no one would laugh at me.*
*They laugh to scare me but what I*
*Could put on canvas would scare them!*
*Like the deep dark canyons or the*
*Blinding explosions when*
*I close my eyes.*

*I must warn you, dear, that they*
*Won't let me come to you.*
*To go outside, to see the trees and*
*Feel the wind and lose myself in the*
*Sky is forbidden me. I'm kept*
*Inside with only walls and one small*
*Window that has bars. What can they*
*Fear from me?*

*I know they plot and plan*
*To do away with me. They*
*Listen to my thoughts. They*

*Pry into my soul. They come into*
*My room like fog. Grey fog. Grey*
*Before black. Black like a hole.*
*Black like a grave. I am not*
*Safe here, Cor, for all their*
*Care. My head is bursting with the*
*Things I know, the pain of things*
*I see. Please come but*
*                Oh, my dear, be careful!*

## Indian Peaches

In midsummer when the Ozark peach orchards hung heavy with ripening fruit, Mrs. Richardson, our dear next-door neighbor, used to hold her annual house party and canning bee at her ancestral home in Cane Hill, about twenty-five miles southwest of Fayetteville. Mother always took Jimmie and me, Mrs. Harding brought Mary Frances and arranged to leave Arthur at home; sometimes other families, the Bates, perhaps, joined the group. Once there, the women plunged into an orgy of blanching, peeling, slicing, or chunking the golden peaches, then pickling them, canning them for winter desserts, or making the imperfect slices up into jam or peach "honey." The children, if they were big enough, carried bushel baskets, took peels and pits to the compost pile, and entertained themselves in various ways. The orchards were rich with spent ammunition from the Civil War Battle of Cane Hill, as well as Indian relics from primitive times. The clear shallow stream was a very favorite place for wading or just lying on the

sandy bottom, noses barely above water. We children
thought that heaven must be very like Cane Hill.

## *Indian Peaches—Cane Hill*

*Indian peaches are the best for pickling.*
*Small, compact, blushing to blood red as they ripen,*
*fitting perfectly into the cup of the waiting hand,*
*placed without bruising in a split basket and,*
*still warm from the fragrant orchard,*
*carried by the men, gleaming*
*with sweat and mad with itching,*
*to the summer kitchen under the shade*
*of tall black walnut trees.*

*Sweet-sour syrup,*
*heady aroma of warring elements,*
*brown sugar and vinegar*
*attended by perfume of spices,*
*sharp ginger, cloves, and pungent cinnamon,*
*bubbles in gluttonous kettles*
*waiting to receive the mellow fruit*
*that's lost its skin in boiling water.*

*Our mothers, cousins, honorary aunts*
*in canning aprons, shapeless and bare-armed,*
*hair curling into springy tendrils*
*from the steam of stove and weather,*
*stir in still more sugar,*
*laugh at their hot dripping faces,*
*shoo us out from underfoot.*

*With what relief I scuttle away*
*from that foaming pickling syrup,*
*too heavily sweet for me.*
*The orchard calls, though the Indian peaches*
*are safe from our sated appetites.*
*Treasures lie hidden in the sandy loam*
*under the trees.*
*Snub-nosed bullets from*
*the War between the States*
*often stub our toes,*
*remind us of the Battle of Cane Hill*
*fought through earlier orchards on these tranquil slopes.*
*Stranger and less frequent*
*are the flinty arrowheads*
*shot long ago by Indian hunters*
*on the trail of game.*

*But soon the peach fuzz settles on our skin.*
*Howling with discomfort,*
*we race to the stream*
*shallow, rippling in the sun.*
*Minnows glint against the sandy bottom.*
*We wade first across then up and down*
*and scarcely feel the quiet current*
*comforting our legs,*
*but we thrill to the tiny eager mouths*
*of the minnows*
*nibbling at our calves.*

*Slowly the summer sun goes down.*
*A thin grey twilight*
*glittering with fireflies begins.*
*Supper is called and we go in.*

*There on board shelves*

*stand the Indian peaches*
*row on row*
*shining in syrup*
*waiting for winter.*

## Wagon Treats

A prime delight of Leverett Street was the ice cream wagon, red and white, small and high-wheeled like a mailman's cart, one of the last horse-drawn vehicles in our Ozark town. When we heard the clear silver of the vendor's bell float down the street and the call, "Ice cream! Pick your flavor—vanilla, chocolate, strawberry!" we started to run toward the nearest adult, hands outstretched, eyes eager—there was little need for words! The grownups had heard the same bell and were already digging into trouser pockets, rummaging through handbags and purses for the nickels we would need. And often they came, too, standing with us in the red dust of the summer street, which ran like blood in the gutters after a thunderstorm, while we called out our choices, well-adorned with Pleases and Thank Yous and an occasional, "mighty nice." Once in a long time there would be a special treat, Jimmie's favorite fresh peach, but I *always* chose chocolate and could be sure it would be there for me. The cones were piled high, and it required a certain skill to lick carefully around the top of the cone and then over the mound of ice cream to push it more firmly into its holder. Sometimes the frozen treat was so cold that it made my teeth and nose ache—small matter!

Although the postman arrived twice daily, rain or shine, summer or winter, his cart was not exciting. After all, he only brought letters and the occasional package, and his cart was smaller and painted a dark, bottle-green. The horses that pulled these carts were slow and steady, accustomed to frequent stops on the same unchanging routes. How startled we were one evening in the twilight to hear the fast clop-clop of hooves and see our trusty mail cart being hurried back to the stables by a trotting mare, hungry for oats and her own stall.

The iceman had a horse-drawn wagon with a sort of cabin on top over the ice and a black oilcloth curtain divided into hanging strips, each about eight inches wide. Mother had a square card to put in the window that told how much ice we wanted that day. Divided into diagonal quadrants, the card showed the black numerals—5, 10, 25, and 50—against a field of yellow. Quickly reading the order, the iceman reached behind the curtain and with his gleaming ice tongs drew out a chunk of solid ice— the right size. Once in a while, when he had to chip ten pounds or so with his sharp pick from a big block, he would give us a handful of chips from the bed of the wagon. Mother liked to have us run into the kitchen and wash our ice chips under running water, but if they had not picked up too much sawdust from the wagonbed, we neglected that nicety. The ice was so clear it had to be clean, was the way we reasoned. Mother was particular, too, in her demand that the ice delivered to her be in one large chunk, not two, so that it would melt more slowly in the big oak icebox that had to be emptied of water every night. If we were having a party, the extra ice chunk sat in a big galvanized washtub covered with gunnysacks. She often ordered extra ice to make our own ice cream in the hand-turned freezer.

Our milk was delivered in an asthmatic Model-T Ford that sat mournfully coughing at the curb while the milkman ran up to the porch with our daily delivery— three or four quarts of whole milk and a bottle of rich cream. When the order included butter, a note requesting it stuck in the mouth of one of the waiting "empties," he ran back to the car and then rang the bell. Otherwise, we "watched for the milk," a duty that often fell to me if I wasn't in school. I didn't like milk and felt that Mother was awfully fussy in her insistence on keeping it as cold as possible. It was surely cold enough once when the milk had been delivered early on a freezing day. It froze in the bottles, pushing plugs of solid yellow cream, each crowned with a cardboard cap, up out of the glass containers. Daddy pointed out to us the graphic expansion of liquid when it freezes, and we marveled that it hadn't spilled over.

Vegetables and fruits came to our house in wagons, sometimes beautifully displayed in shelves that slanted down from a middle ridge but often in open wagon beds. This was especially true of the corn and melon wagons—piles of green cobs to pull open and check for freshness of the yellow and white kernels and the presence or absence of worms. My favorite and my father's was Country Gentleman with its small, uneven, white rows, but as an occasional treat we had regular field corn picked young and tender, although its kernels were much larger than sweet corn and had tough skins. A quarter bought at least a dozen ears.

The melon wagon had hay or straw bedding for the lush, ripe fruit. The watermelons were huge, displaying many shades of green: dark, almost black, light emerald, and chartreuse, as well as delicious striped "rattlesnake melons." Some were fat and almost round, some long and so slender that a slice would fit perfectly on a dinner plate. Always the farmer who brought them by offered to "plug" the melon. This meant a quick square or triangular cut into the melon itself and a chance to taste the pulled-out plug, carefully gauging its ripeness, color, and texture. The hollow sound of the melon when it was spanked like a baby or rapped with the knuckles was a guarantee against too many being plugged and rejected.

Muskmelons, or "mushmelons" in colloquial talk, were harder to judge. Larger than cantaloupes and much coarser in texture, they were checked for color of webbing or base, weight, and aroma. Smaller cantaloupes, the size of giant oranges, were sniffed and pressed on the stem end for "give." It fascinated me to see my father and the farmer heft and discard one fruit after another until they reached agreement on the chosen one. Daddy always picked out the melons and bought three or six at a time.

Mother chose smaller fruits and vegetables from other vendors. Shiny red and yellow tomatoes, Kentucky wonder beans that broke with a crisp crack, proving their freshness, creamy wax beans, butter beans, green pea pods to crack open and free of their contents with a thumb, hard heads of cabbage, leafy lettuce, pointed pods of okra (which I hated) were usually arranged on one side of the stepped display shelves; on the other side small fruits held forth: greengage, red, and purple plums; pie cherries, smaller and tarter than Bings or Royal Annes; grapes in season, always Concords, occasionally Thompson's seedless; apples—from spring pippins to autumn McIntosh, Jonathan, red or golden Delicious (we lived in apple country); pears and many different kinds of peaches: Elbertas, Hales, and Indian, were only a few of the varieties available. In the summer, berries of all kinds—strawberries dripping juicily in their baskets; black caps for my father and the paler red raspberries, my mother's choice; loganberries; rich bold blackberries—stood ready for the table or the canning kitchen. There were no oranges, grapefruit, or bananas. Those were sold at the grocery store and were special treats in short supply. Unlike our local juice-laden fruits, they came from faraway places and were often packed in sawdust.

The fragrance of the mingled fruits was truly heavenly. Warmed by the sun, the fruits gave off their sweetest aroma, deepened at times by a hint of spoilage since morning. A heavy undertone like a musical continuum was the grassy garden smell of the vegetables, and once in a while an over-ripe tomato made a statement all its own.

Fayetteville air was full of traceable odors and few were unpleasant. Clean and high (about 2,600 feet), with no manufacturing, it was home to many fragrant gardens. Sweet peas and roses, honeysuckle and lilies grew beside my favorites, lilies-of-the-valley and tuberoses. The scent of nicotiana and magnolia at night was almost overpowering. On Children's Day, when we all brought bouquets of flowers to church, the perfume of roses, lilacs, lilies, and catalpa blossoms was almost too heavy for breathing.

Down in Shuler Town by the station, the stench of coal-fed locomotives, cinders, and soot had its own peculiar charm. You knew you were somewhere different, set apart. You had to be careful. And when you went by the cannery across from the National cemetery and the nauseous stink of tomatoes, crate after crate after crate, filled your nostrils, you started to run or hurry your pace so that you'd inhale the least possible amount of that tainted air. The railroad tracks ran down beside the cannery, but we never stopped there at our favorite trestle to make doll scissors by leaving crossed pins on the tracks for the heavy wheels to flatten when the cannery was in operation. Was it from the cannery that the noon whistle blew? A spike of sound that split the heavens with its sharpness, it cleanly separated morning from afternoon and marked our need to get on with the day.

On the Fourth of July and to a lesser extent on Christmas, the smell of gunpowder and assorted fireworks was heavy in the air. The odor of punk, with which we lit our Roman candles, sky rockets, and crackers, was especially rank. And mixed with the circular flare of pinwheels, the crackle of hot foot on the pavement, and the acrid burning wire of sparklers was the intoxication of playing with fire—man's friend or enemy.

# Three

# A House of My Own

## Look Back

TO THOSE she loves, she'll laugh and tell how that warm summer day was sweet with jasmine, how the freshly watered grass pulled at her slippers, how hard it was to keep so still—she who climbed trees to sew her dollclothes. Unseen but seeing, in her swaying perch, she shaped her scraps of linen, gingham, silk and watched the world pass by.

She stands there in the silvered shadow of the giant maple dressed in her best—white, embroidered petticoat starched and ruffled to billow out over thin white-stockinged legs firmly planted in shining Mary Janes. Long brown curls are caught by a taffeta bow, enormous butterfly that's landed just a shade off the middle of her head.

Memory says the bow was yellow to match her sash.

Laddie sits quietly under her left hand. Fresh from a bath, his splendid ruff of white reflects the sun.

It's an occasion.

The photographer, Mr. Fields, dives in and out of his small black tent, fixing forever a nine-year-old held in this leafy frame.

## A House of My Own

When I was eight years old, we moved from the sprawling white house on Leverett Street across town in Fayetteville to Dickson Street, and I came into my own house. What could be grander?

My house had been part of the old servants' quarters behind the Big House. My parents converted the down-stairs of the two-story structure to storage and gave me the undivided upstairs room for a playhouse. When I climbed the outside stairway and opened the narrow door to my own retreat, I was in a world apart. The dusty fragrance of its still air gave way for a while to the smell of Naptha soap on the floorboards, kerosene and vinegar on the windows as everything was scrubbed and brought to a state of cleanliness of which my mother could approve. I rather liked the earlier scent even though it tickled my nose and made me sneeze, but I was glad to have the spider webs swept away.

The roof slanted sharply to the floor from the high ridgepole that ran from gable to gable over facing windows. The height of mid-ceiling made wonderful shadows (as well as extra cobwebs) where the slope almost touched the floor. Mother had Elizabeth, our hired girl, wash and starch some old curtains for the two windows, one facing my room in the Big House, one overlooking the tall cornrows in Will Carr's vegetable garden. If I pressed close enough to that window and looked slant-wise out through the glass, I could just see the three box-like structures that were my father's bee hives. Beside the garden window, a cracked mirror hung on the wall. An old rocker beside an apple crate gave me a place to rock my dolls or read. A red plush hassock with an un-trustworthy leg completed the furnishings, except for my dressup trunk pushed under the eaves and a battery of fruit crates (we lived in apple country) that could magically become whatever I needed: bookcases, chests of drawers, tables, chairs, even a stove if I wanted to pretend-cook my graham crackers and Delicious apples.

It never occurred to me to ask for, or even to miss, a bed. My dolls slept in apple boxes when they visited from my own bedroom, but I took it for granted that when I was called to supper, I would say goodbye to my house and go to eat and spend the night in my parents' home.

But, oh, the dressing-up from the depths of the cavernous trunk! One of my favorites, a mossy green ribbed-silk basque trimmed with heavy braid, I had loved since I was three, a little girl in Kansas. Then there were Mother's grey French kid oxfords with stiletto toes and baby French heels. One of those ornately curved heels had broken, but I could almost make up for it by walking on tiptoe.

Dickson Street, as the house was always identified by the family, had other delights than my playhouse. The lofty stable and stableyard were a country all to themselves. There was the high swing tree and the enormous old syringa bushes, their perfume so sweet that it put me to sleep when I lay on the grass beside them to read. Yucca plants with their towering candelabras of blossoms stood near the corner of the terrace and tall hollyhocks reached up under my second floor window. Rose bushes blossomed everywhere, and their scent was carried into the Big House where the cut flowers decorated tables and mantles in dining room, parlor and hall.

The wide veranda was floored with narrow boards so tightly laid that I could roller-skate in long smooth strokes and practice turns and hard braking after a race around the corner of the house. Skating there when it rained, I could smell the freshly laid dust in the street.

A flowering vine that draped the veranda had joints in the dry stems about three inches apart, just right for play cigarettes. My new playmates, mostly boys, and I broke them into appropriate lengths, lit them, inhaled deeply as we had observed Pola Negri and Rudolph Valentino do in Saturday matinees, and gasped for help. The long cells in the stems ran open from joint to joint and we drew in pure flame from the tip. Undaunted but with blistered tongues, we tried again and again to master the art of sophisticated smoking. No one could have convinced us that real smokers were not flame swallowers, as well.

## Vision of Identity

I did my full share of dreaming as a child. Everything could be made into something else if you just looked at it differently. Sometimes it helped to be sick. Fever-struck hot eyes turned to the ceiling, I lost myself in the silver patterns scrawled across the ivory paper. Angels, dragons, baby buggies, steeples formed and reformed. Sometimes they moved toward me, sometimes away. Hiding under the sheet didn't help; when I peeked out they were there. As my fever rose, I felt that I floated up into them, but then they receded. Heaven, I was sure, must be like that—indistinguishable silvery forms, unattainable. When I grew cooler, I would ask about their mysterious appearance and disappearance. Until then it would be my secret.

Secrets, too, were in the sleeping porch, where fluffy featherbeds smothered me on summer nights. Lying alone, watching the pattern of stars flicker through the screen, I sometimes saw a torrent of falling stars. But they would never fall on me. It was my porch, my house, my sky. No one could know my magic, feel my power.

Outside on a spring day, I could lie in the grass and look up into blue blue sky ornamented with huge cumulus clouds. That's what Daddy said they were. To me they looked like enormous blobs of whipped cream or high-beaten egg whites for a meringue or an angel food cake. Some were as solid as mashed potatoes, and when the sun shone in just the right place behind them, I could see the golden butter melt down the sides. If heaven was up there, maybe the clouds were what angels ate! Or maybe that was the way angels traveled. With wind pushing them across the sky, they often seemed to be chasing each other. What a way to ride! What a view!

Somehow, I always seemed to fall asleep or lose focus before I figured any of this out. Could I be seen, I wondered, or would I look smaller than an ant to an angel on a cloud? I had little sense of myself in relation to the world at large until one day in my father's library when I was prowling through his childhood schoolbooks. An old McGuffey's Reader, dog-eared and worn, fell open in my hands. There on the fly leaf, written in a childish but careful script, it said:

James Ralph Jewell
Moran School
Morantown
Allen County
State of Kansas
United States of America
Continent of North America
Western Hemisphere
The Planet Earth
The Universe

I was stunned. My father had known who he was when he was a little boy. I had seen the tiny Moran School where he and my mother had met as classmates. They both knew who they were, where they belonged in the order of things. I tried it for myself:

Margaret Elaine Jewell
Peabody School
University of Arkansas
Fayetteville
Washington County
State of Arkansas

That much was different for me and then I joined my father as an American, a world citizen, part of the universe. At least for then, I knew who I was, where I belonged!

## Bed Time

My parents were great believers in the healing powers of sleep—especially for their children. The hour of seven-thirty in the evening, summer and winter, was observed as sacred in our home, and I was ready to start to high school before a slightly later hour of eight o'clock was set for me, to the freely expressed envy of my brother, four years younger. My own feeling was one of well-deserved prestige—rarely equalled since.

Mother or Daddy would simply announce in a pleasant but authoritative manner, "Children, it is seven-thirty," and we knew that protest, pleading, or tantrums would be in vain. The hour had struck. Getting a drink was a last resource, so off we went to the kitchen—milk for Jimmie, water for me. And then it was back to the dining room or living room for our goodnight hug and kiss from each parent.

Jimmie usually went first because he was the younger, and that was fine with me because it offered a few moments to get from the refrigerator my surreptitious treat, a Red Delicious apple. Unfortunately this was not encouraged at bedtime because we were not supposed to eat in bed or to eat anything after we had brushed our teeth. They were to remain in pristine condition, inviolate throughout the night, when, it was believed, tooth decay lurked, waiting to strike the careless brusher. Daytime apples were encouraged and, since we lived in apple country, were always available—the one between-meals snack we could have without asking.

My efforts to think out this problem focussed on having my apple without "worrying" my parents, and I had evolved a plan that worked successfully for some time. It consisted of slipping the apple inside one leg of my full-white bloomers and keeping it somehow between my thighs so that it would not be felt when Mother, seated in her low chair, put her arm around me. (Daddy tended to hug me higher up.) My gait was not exactly normal as I waddled around saying goodnight, but my parents never challenged me, in spite of several near-misses that sent my heart rate shooting up. Did they know? I have often wondered about it because they consistently outsmarted me. My father and I were very much alike, and he had a sixth sense as far as I was concerned. My mother, when asked about it in later years, smiled and said, "Honey, parents must be careful not to see everything."

Safely embraced and sent off to bed where I planned to read and eat my forbidden fruit, I faced the tall, curving steps in the hall. In summer I raced up, went through my parents' bedroom, and entered mine at the back of the house. It led into the big screened porch where I slept from May to October—a wonderful place to lie and dream, look out into the giant maples and try to count falling stars when it got darker.

But in the winter when it was dark, the stairwell seemed cavernous and full of threat in spite of the downstairs hall lights. There was no two-way switch and I had to climb all the way up to the second floor where I could stand on tiptoe outside my parents' door and pull the cord (made of tiny metal beads) that would light the upstairs hall. Torn between terror of the shadows and a stubborn pride in my own self-reliance, I worked out another plan. As I started up the stairs, I began a bold rendition of "Jesus Loves Me" with special emphasis on "This I know." Surely He would let no harm come to a small girl so loudly affirming her faith. It worked! To this day, I have got safely to bed every night of my life.

## Violet

Violet came to be my friend shortly after our move to the broad-verandaed stucco, sitting high on its terrace above Dickson Street. She had first been my imaginary companion when I was an "only" little girl in Kansas before my brother's birth. I was Rose to match her Violet, and I still have a postcard sent to me by my father (away on a speaking trip) on which he wrote, "Dear Rose, How are you and how is Violet? Tell her I asked about her. . . Love, Daddy." Now I was lonely again. Mary Frances, my best friend, who lived conveniently across the street on Leverett, had been left behind. I saw her only at

school and on especially arranged visits. Even Mildred
Williams, who bullied and fascinated me, was not close
at hand. My brother spent all of his time with Hagan,
the new freckle-faced neighbor next door. They were four
years younger, anyway, and it showed my forlorn state
that I would even consider them as possible companions.

So I spent most of my time alone after school and on
weekends, swinging high into the branches of the big
maple (not as good for climbing as the familiar leafy retreat I had left on Leverett but with a superior swing
branch) or roller-skating on the veranda. (I was still forbidden sidewalk skating on the busy boulevard.)

I read more and more: in the back parlor where the
glass-fronted bookcases held my parents' books, nearly
buried in my featherbed on the screened porch, or in my
bedroom where I could lay my book aside and see visions
of castles and clouds in the abstract swirls of the satin-
moire ceiling paper. OR, I could play DOLLS. Between
the mirrored wardrobe and the window, my parents had
built a spacious doll-house. Using wooden packing-boxes
for rooms, they stacked a honeycomb that was a bit taller
than I against the wall so that the ceiling of the upstairs
bedrooms was slightly above my head. The height
pleased me; it was inappropriate, I thought, to look
down on the roof of a house! Each room had been carefully papered in miniature designs chosen from free
"end rolls" at the paint and wallpaper store. The ceiling
papers were similar to that in my own room, the floors
were heavy brown wrapping paper or, in the kitchen and
bathroom, oilcloth that looked like linoleum. There were
three bedrooms to accommodate parents, brothers, and
sisters, one bath, kitchen, dining room, parlor/living
room and a big porch. My dolls and I were very happy
there.

And we were even happier when a low bookcase between the windows on an adjacent wall became the modest home for Stanley, boy friend of the resident doll family, who could now live with his parents "around the corner." It was important to be able to visit back and forth.

Violet appeared one rainy afternoon and immediately took charge of Stanley, his home, and his goings and comings. I was not surprised by her appearance and relished being able to talk about what the doll families had planned for the day and how they should be dressed. "He can't wear his suit," she said with scorn, "they're only going on a picnic!" So, off came the offensive Sunday garments and on went a ragtag pair of denim pants. After a bit more advice from her, I had my family in loose aprons and shifts, bathing suits rolled up and ready to go. Doll outings under a window had no need to fear either rain or ants! We had a great picnic on buttered graham crackers and an apple, filched from a quick trip downstairs to the kitchen. Elizabeth, our hired girl/cook, was having a brief rest in her room.

Violet loved to sit beside me on the bench as I pedaled out stirring or romantic music on the player piano. She chose "Stars and Stripes Forever" or the "Washington Post March" in counterpoint to my favorites: "Traumerei" or the "Barcarolle" from *Tales of Hoffman*. We both loved "Humoresque" and repeated sotto voce the doggerel lyrics:

> *Apple pie without the cheese*
> *Is like a kiss without the squeeze*
> *Te da de da...*

It was wonderful to have someone to giggle with, to confide in, to leave the piano with and lie on our stomachs listening to Caruso's and Schumann-Heink's commanding voices on the Victrola.

When the weather was good, we stood up and pumped together in the swing, almost disappearing as the arc rose higher and higher. We made clover chains for ourselves and catalpa bonnets for our smallest dolls. Often when called in to supper, I would tell Mother that Violet was staying for the evening meal and Mother would welcome her, suggest that we both go off and wash our hands, ask Elizabeth to set an extra plate beside mine at the table. I used to wonder why Elizabeth often went off to the kitchen, shaking her head and muttering under her breath.

Mother and Daddy were very understanding and polite to Violet. My brother, Jimmie, was openly scoffing, refused to say a simple hello, even asked impudent questions about what she looked like or whether she looked like anything. Challenged, I probably said that she looked like me: same age, same size, perhaps with long curls and skinny legs. She was a personality, a presence, a much-needed playmate, who often spoke tartly and was not reluctant to give an opinion. But she sensed what I thought, said, hoped and dreamed. Who could ask for more in a companion?

Strangely enough, Violet never seemed to be around when I was playing "dress-up" and living that other life in my servants' quarter playhouse. She never played in the barn or jumped from the hay window when neighborhood kids showed off to each other. And as I spent more time with new friends, Violet visited me less often.

Her departure was dramatic. One late afternoon when I had played alone in my room after school, Mother heard a startled cry, followed by the thumping-rolling sound of a falling body. She ran to the front hall just in time to see me come tumbling down the circular stairway and end up pulling myself to a sitting position on the bottom step. I glared up at the top of the stairs.

"She pushed me!" I told my amazed mother in a voice of pure fury. "Violet pushed me!" I repeated, incredulous at such action from a trusted friend. "I will NEVER play with her again!"

And I never did!

## The Perfume Bottle

It was one of the first things that I knew I wanted to have when I grew up, a symbol of status in that magical world to come. Standing on the small right hand bracket of my mother's chest of drawers, it balanced the picture of my father on the opposite side of the oval mirror. Its cut glass globe was about the size of a fat pear but the sharpness of its edges discouraged holding. It was at its best when the sun caught and splintered on every edge of its design and threw prisms of color all around the room. The perfume bottle always held French violet eau de cologne, a delicate green that made a pale contrast to its flashing rainbows.

As I lay on Mother's bed or on the floor watching her dress, the arcs of colored light would shoot from the perfume bottle and she would tip the cologne onto her hands and then stroke my hair back from my forehead, the clean fresh scent of violets completing the spell that kept me dreaming of all that was still to come.

## Sleep-Lacing

I can still remember my rage, the sullen frustration of perceived injustice. My parents' memory was of a different sort. They had been reading in the library downstairs, contentedly relaxed at the end of a demanding day, both children now safely asleep. Noises from my room, directly above, alerted them: a door swung open, closed, sounds of muffled footsteps and then the continuous low murmur of an angry voice.

They hurried up the curving stairs and through their bedroom, from which they could see lights in my room, the door half-open. Sitting on the blanket chest at the foot of her big bed was their nine-year-old daughter, still in her long, full, winter nightgown, bent over and furiously lacing her shoes. It was obvious that I was still asleep, they told me afterward, and they stood quietly at the open door, reluctant to wake me but eager to prevent any disastrous move.

And as they watched, they listened. I was enraged with them, they gathered from my muttered monologue. My accusations went on and on as I thrust the shoestrings through eyelet after eyelet in my new pair of high-topped shoes, the pride of my wardrobe and my life at that time. Brought from Chicago by my father, who had been away on a speaking trip, they were a soft, lustrous brown leather with tops of fine khaki-colored serge and far outshone the customary black winter shoes my friends and I usually wore. But now they were the objects of my hot anger.

I seemed to believe that I had been rousted out of bed by unfeeling parents who demanded that I lace my shoes clear to the top in order to prove that I was worthy of caring for such treasures. As I jabbed each metal tip through another hole and jerked the lacing tight, I looked across at the mirrored wardrobe door which faced my blanket chest, as much as to say, "You poor put-upon child!"

One shoe was laced up; I started on the other, poking, pulling and tightening, complaining with every breath, "They would make me do something like this. 'Lace your shoes,' they said. 'Let's see if you can do it'!" I got within two or three holes of the top of the second shoe and then in total fury cried out, "That's enough!" and began to tear the laces out of the holes to open up the shoes. My face was flushed, my hair fairly stood out from my head, my whole body bent to the task of undoing the hated assignment.

It was too much for my parents, watching from the door. A low chuckle escaped them. I jumped to my feet, seeing them apparently for the first time, and screamed, "Don't make fun of me!" As they rushed forward, I burst into sobs.

And there my memory ends. According to their story, I was comforted, my shoes were unlaced and set back in the wardrobe, and I was lifted into bed where I fell back to sleep.

## Finders, Keepers

Some people are just born lucky. My brother was one of those, especially at finding things. With no effort at all, he picked up Indian head pennies, shiny nickels, once even a heavy half-dollar. He seldom came home from a walk across the campus or down through Shuler Town, past the station, without finding a few coins in the grass or shining on the sidewalk. My friends seemed to have something of this talent and flourished four leaf clovers or "lucky pennies" they had made their own.

I was not what friends of my parents identified as "an observant child" although I stoutly maintained that I looked at what I wanted to see. I'm sure that I spent more time in dreaming than in looking down at the ground, but I did SO long for the excitement and status of a Great Find.

My luck was to change when I was about ten. One fine day, passing the luxuriant hedge of the house next door, I saw a small yellow box waiting in the shadows for someone to pick it up. It was clean and new, identified by the printing on the cover as a J and P Coates Sewing Thread box, the size to hold twelve spools. I had seen similar boxes on my mother's White sewing machine. Two crossed rubber bands held the box securely shut.

I was less than thrilled over the idea of spools of thread as my treasure but snapped off the elastics to discover what colors might have come my way. The box lay heavier in my hand than sewing cotton and the open lid revealed something carefully packed in pink tissue paper. What could it be? I pulled the wrapping aside and fairly jumped in amazement when a pair of gleaming false teeth grinned up at me from a bed of absorbent cotton.

They appeared to be brand new, the glittering white porcelain incisors shining like pearls against the rich pink gums. No one I knew had ever displayed such a treasure! I thought at once of what a splendid addition they would be to my dress-up finery. How surprised my father would be when I opened my mouth and these gorgeous dentures made their debut!

Tucking the pink paper back around my findings, I snapped the box shut and ran back home to my special playhouse. There I took the teeth out for closer inspection, marveled again at their pristine condition and went over to the mirror to try them on.

Somehow that proved hard to do. They looked enormous and, when I tried to span them with my fingers, seemed plenty big enough to fit over my own native, less glamorous set. I opened my mouth—WIDE—but as I brought the false teeth closer, my jaw traitorously started to close. The little muscles at the joints tightened and I thought I was going to be sick.

Clearly, I needed help, so once again I packed my beauties and ran down the steps and across the lawn to the Big House. Mother was upstairs in the sewing room and knew when she saw me that something was up. But she was just as amazed as I had been when the J and P Coates box disgorged its contents. "Honey girl!" she gasped.

Then as she listened to my dreams of dressing up in my dental finery, she became more serious, complimented me on having brought them to her, explained my strange reluctance to actually install them in my own mouth as a matter of taste and sensitivity. Finally she asked me how I thought the previous owner would get along without them, suggested that I find the evening paper and search the want ads. Sure enough, right there in the *Fayetteville Democrat* under "Lost" was a plea for the return of the dentures and, to my extreme satisfaction, it said, "Reward."

Mother made the call and a relieved male voice announced that the owner (of both teeth and voice) would be at our house before dinner time. The hour that passed was a long one for me, but I conjured up wild dreams of possible rewards. At the ring of the bell, I flew to the door, Mother close behind.

A fine looking elderly man asked, "Are you the little girl who found my teeth?" He neither lisped nor garbled.

Clearly a man of means, he must have had two sets of teeth—perhaps good for a hundred dollars reward?

I nodded and handed him the package. He opened the box (the pink tissue was beginning to look a little worn) and smiled as he drew out a black wallet. My heart throbbed. What would a hundred dollar bill look like?

Then to my utter astonishment, I heard my mother say, "Oh no, you mustn't. Margaret is only too happy to have been of some service to you."

The gentleman inclined his head, bent and kissed my hand, said, "Thank you very much, my dear," and went down the front steps and away.

Mother was astounded by the tears that gushed forth the instant the door closed, clear evidence that Margaret was not at all happy. She explained a totally adult view of pleasure in doing for others. Daddy announced when he came home and heard the story that my allowance for the following week would be doubled for exemplary service, but that fell far short of a hundred dollars, and I hadn't even tried on the teeth!

## Night Terror

My balance was precarious, perched on a spine of rock thrusting up from the sluggish water. I had to escape but I was frozen in place. Even the scream I needed to call for help was stuck in my tightening throat. How long could I stay above the water on these treacherous, slippery rocks?

I had to stay; below in the heavy slime that slushed around jagged stones, as black as the one I clung to, were snakes. Snakes of all sizes. Snakes of all colors.

Snakes whose iridescence shone from the mud. Snakes so dull and brown that they looked like the mud in motion. Snakes that reared their spade-like heads and darted venomous tongues. Snakes that rolled and coiled and fell back on themselves. Snakes that seemed to yawn like cottonmouths, exposing a mass of soft white tissue. Snakes thin as whips, enormous snakes looping their firehose-sized bodies like boa constrictors. Green snakes, purple snakes, brown and black and copper snakes—all fanged and ready for me to slip. The green, hooded eyes told me this: much as they writhed and slithered from rock to water, they kept those glinting eyes on me.

The foulness of the snake pit dizzied me. The hiss of the reptiles buzzed in my ears. I slipped, recovered, slipped again, fell on all fours, dodged back from the lash of a triangular head. I must get out. I fell again. A shining loop, black as the rock it circled, spun toward me. I slipped—

I woke.

I had had my bad dream again. I was sobbing, wet with sweat, panting in terror. Could I call out? Would someone hear?

All through my childhood, this terrible dream recurred. Always I woke in my own bed, in my familiar room, was held and comforted. But never in my dream could I remember this and never could I stop it. The fearful scenario, once started, played relentlessly through to the end.

## Special Delivery

Snowstorms were rare in the Ozarks. Some winters passed with no snow at all, only thin crusts of ice over the mud puddles to mark a freezing night. When it did snow heavily enough for a sled to be used, the city closed most of the streets with a steep grade so that the town's young people could safely enjoy the unusual pleasures of real winter. (Known as the Athens of the Ozarks, Fayetteville was a miniature San Francisco.) We brought out seldom-used heavy coats then, mittens, stocking caps for show and donned long-sleeved, long-legged underwear that was carefully concealed. I well remember how hard it was to fold the ankles of my long johns tightly and smoothly enough so that I could pull my ribbed black stockings over them. It was a real art.

I must have been nine or ten the winter that a heavy fall of snow began late in the morning as we watched from the broad school windows and saw the campus rapidly disappear under that fresh white blanket. School was an experimental one directed by the University of Arkansas College of Education. Classes were small enough that only even-numbered grades were taught one year and odd numbers the next. In that way a youngster starting in first grade could be assured of orderly progress through the eight grades before high school. If you skipped a grade, however, you had to skip two—say from third to fifth. There was little skipping. Our classmates became members of an extended family and were close enough to support, challenge, criticize, and discourage any showing-off in one another.

Mrs. Simpson quickly turned the opportune storm into a science lesson. It justified our standing at the windows, talking about why it was snow we saw rather than rain, questioning what could happen to make it turn to hail and, before long, she maneuvered us to our desks to cut or draw as many different snowflakes as we could remember or imagine. Mrs. Simpson was full of good ideas, and the only thing I regretted about going to Peabody was that we didn't march in and out as they did in public school. That marching had a certain style, I felt, that our informal "You may go now" lacked.

As I drew six-pointed shapes and learned to fold paper for cutting into thirds, I began to wonder about lunch. The weather had been quite pleasant when I walked to school and I had planned, as usual, to walk home again with my father for lunch. Mother was a great believer in hot meals, and I seldom had the treat of taking a packed lunch to school. Daddy was Dean of Education, and his offices were on the top floor of the building where I went to school. This proximity held both advantages and disadvantages, I had learned, but walking to the campus and back with Daddy was a real bonus. The feel of his finely-boned hand closing over mine, the freedom to talk and ask questions about everything in the world made our daily walks pure delight. I almost regretted the after-school trips home with my friends, giggling and teasing Helen Oakley, whose mother had bought her TWO copies of Frye's *Geography*, so that she wouldn't have to carry the big green book home and back. We didn't especially like carrying our own books, but we alternately looked down on Helen as being hopelessly spoiled and envied her that position. We could have fun this afternoon, I thought, wading through the snow, maybe making "angels" in its smooth surface.

Lunch time came sooner than I had anticipated, and I ran upstairs, coat over my arm, to see what Daddy would say about lunch. His secretary, Miss Lano, looked up from her typewriter to greet me. Spellbound, I watched her beautiful white hands play over the keys. Someday, I hoped, I would be a secretary! On her right hand she wore a large square-cut amethyst in a massive gold setting that fascinated me. Once she told me that the ring had been her father's. I felt a slight disappointment when I looked at my father's more modest sapphire set in black enamel.

But as he came smiling out of his office, I knew that something special was going to happen—and it did. "We are going to stay here for lunch today, Margaret," he told me. "Your mother called just a few minutes ago. She has a surprise."

Mother loved surprises and special treats and holidays. For someone who always seemed to know the right and conventional way to behave, she had an amazing capacity for celebration and in my father she had a willing and creative accomplice. Now he led me to his office windows and suggested that I watch closely through the white curtain of snow. It was still falling densely over the deserted campus. Everyone had taken refuge inside. No—not everyone. I seemed to see a gray shadow moving across the ROTC parade ground, going under the double rows of maples along Senior Walk, coming out into the open toward Peabody Hall. As the shadow came closer, it took shape. Snowflakes fell on Mother's heavy velour hat, made white epaulets on the shoulders of her warm navy coat. The beaver collar was turned up around her ears and neck. She carried a big picnic basket cushioned with snow.

Daddy took my hand and we ran down two flights of steps to meet Mother just as she reached the building's carved front doors. We hugged her at the same time and Daddy kissed her, too. She was laughing and bright-eyed, rosy-cheeked and happy with her plan. We rushed up the stairway again and, after a quick hello to Miss Lano, the three of us fairly danced around my father's office. Mother's coat was hung by the radiator. She touched my cheek to show how cold her hands were and then she spread lunch. She had brought a tea cloth for the table across from the desk and plates and cups and napkins and sandwiches, and there must have been fruit and cookies but I remember best the hot chocolate. Poured from a huge, steaming thermos, topped with whipped cream from a little jar in her basket and sprinkled with cinnamon, it looked and smelled just the way I felt. Mother caught my expression, smiled at the success of her surprise, and poured me another cup.

## *Railroad Crossing— X —Look Out for the Cars*

It happened on a day when I was walking to school with Blanche and Irene because Daddy was out of town, down-state visiting high schools in his role of advisor to the state accreditation committee. We were a little late as we started to run across the platter of tracks we crossed every day on the way to school or coming home again. Looking right and left to gauge safe distance from the puffing engines, we felt the smooth slipperiness of rails, the rough grain of the paving through our racing shoe soles. North of the Missouri Pacific station, where the stubby switch engines chugged back and forth pulling hyphenated sections of passenger trains and box cars, more than eight pairs of lustreless black parallels crossed the flat of Dickson Street before it rose gently on either side: toward the campus in the west or to Mount Sequoyah, east. The V-shaped switches, set low in sandstone paving blocks and cindery crossties, sent cars off again in new directions.

It happened fast.

That day in March, running as always, I felt my ankle turn, slipped, fell, and found I could not rise. Foot caught by a switching-V, firmly wedged as in a vise, I lay where I had fallen, face down in the gravel. My hands smarted from the grit, one knee burned with pain. And, looking up for help, I saw what I had failed to see before: the black switch-engine bearing down on me, red fire-box glowing, pistons pumping, engineer's face turned backwards to catch a brakeman's signal. He didn't hear the scream of my friends, shrill against the grinding wheels. There was a stench of coal and steam. I pressed into the pavement, desperate to shrink myself, pulling harder to free my captured foot. Closer the engine came, higher and louder the noise. The tracks trembled. I closed my eyes and tried to muster prayers.

Then suddenly I was jerked—apart it felt—and thrown back from the train, stopped by a broken curb. Companions cried. Strangers checked my injured foot and tried to calm my shaking body, to comfort my tears. The stranger who had yanked me loose muttered when questioned, quickly disappeared.

We never knew his name.

Adults must have taken me home. Dr. Ellis checked me over—except for my twisted, swollen foot, my cinder-scraped palms and knee, I was physically uninjured. But the terror of the accident stayed with me for years. To stand on a station platform while a train pulled in: whistle blowing, pistons pumping, wheels sparking on the tracks was impossible for me. I had to wait inside the station and emerge only after the train had screamed to a halt.

Mother and Daddy were understanding and helpful. There was no pressure from them to "forget it," "come on with everyone else." Jimmie, of course, considered me a scaredy cat and, out of my parents' hearing, mocked my fear. But I was allowed to take my time in recovering and now, although I still have the irrational premonition that each engine just might leave its track and come after me, I can stand on the Menlo Park Caltrain platform—looking reasonably calm—and board the commuter coach for The City.

## Dare, Dare, Double Dare

I was slow, it seems to me, in learning that a dare was not an obligation—absolute and almost sacred. Since I was usually younger than my classmates and playmates, I felt a particular need to prove myself by meeting any challenge. One of my hardest lessons was learned in the barnyard of the Dickson Street house.

The barn and barnyard were leased by a construction company of some kind. Stock was seldom stabled in that hard-packed section of the property behind the house, separated from it by lawn and shrubs and shaded by a couple of tall elms. But when the huge draft horses came, they were a source of wonder. Tall, handsome beasts with heavy manes and sturdy flanks and shoulders, they placed their great hooves carefully like moving tree trunks. The pair most often in residence must have been Belgians, bright chestnut with flaxen manes and tails. Only infrequently did we see the matched Percherons, their strong grey necks beaded with sweat. As I remember, the horses stayed overnight only when their owner felt they should not have the long trip home to their own quarters, after and before a hard day's work.

But the loft was kept full of hay for them, and the yard was packed by the blows of their tremendous feet. Our gang of playmates, at the time all boys except myself, made the barn our headquarters for meetings of rapidly forming and dissolving clubs. We explored all the nooks and crannies, being careful to leave everything as we found it in order to preserve our right to trespass. Although there was no farm equipment stored there, it afforded infinite opportunities to climb and hide and swing from beams. It was the other side of my life on Dickson Street. In my own playhouse, I could be alone, live in a fantasy world of being grown-up, have my doll children, and feel accountable to no one but myself. Here in the barnyard, I was part of a group—a little younger and of a different sex, but accepted because I could run faster than most, climb higher, and swing hand over hand from the stable beams.

The acceptance was conditional, I knew, an achievement that caused me considerable tension. I was a fairly daring child and when at any time a modicum of common sense threatened to cancel a challenge, all it took to force my foolhardy nature into command position was a taunting, "Dare you!" from one of the boys. At once I was up and ready to go—to climb from the fence to the top of the barn roof, to shinny up the heavy rope that hung from a hook over the loft door and was used to lift hay from the wagons into the loft.

It was that window into the loft that nearly proved to be my Waterloo. The big square opening was as high off the ground as my second-story window in the Big House. Below it lay hard-packed clay, and we all feared falling as we tried to climb the rope dangling in front of it. One hot afternoon in September, as we lay in the hay trying to forget that school had started, we began to brag. "I'll jump off the landing to the loft if you will," Hayden began.

"That's no trick," Edmund responded. "I'll jump off the roof where it hangs over the fence." Edmund was go-

ing to be an undertaker when he grew up, and we all
thought he had small regard for the duration of life.

"Girls can't jump," said Joe, looking straight at me to
cover up his reluctance to make a higher boast.

"I can! Come on out and see," and I flounced off the
hay and down to the landing, from which I jumped to
the barn floor.

The boys came after me and out to the fence. Edmund
climbed up on the roof as he had promised. It looked
higher than we remembered it, but one after the other
we climbed up and jumped to the ground eight feet or so
below. The clay was like concrete; our knees trembled
and we all looked a little white, but the contest was on.
Where could we find a higher place to jump?

My eyes raised to the loft window. "How about that?" I
pointed.

"Dare you!" Hayden and Joe yelled together.

"I will if you will," came out with a squeak.

"I told you, I told you," Joe taunted. "Scaredy cat, ate
a rat, don't know what she's looking at—"

The pit of my stomach tightened into a knot.

"Dare, dare, double dare, Get up off your rocking
chair," the three boys bellowed in chorus.

Angrily I ran into the barn and flew up the stairs and
across the loft. When I appeared at the window, the
voices dropped for a moment and then with increased
volume: "Dare! Dare! Double dare!"

"Get out of my way!" I screamed and jumped. It was
a long way down and then, suddenly, I landed. My ankle
buckled, my backbone tried to pierce my skull. Stars
were not all I saw. . .

Even my tormentors were quiet and gathered round
to see what the result had been. I pushed them aside and
stood up unaided. Nothing was broken, I decided, but I
did want to be alone. By a great stroke of luck, I heard
Mother's voice calling me to dinner. The gang disap-

peared as if by magic. I staggered toward the house and went into the little bathroom at the end of the porch. Suddenly I had a desperate need to go to the toilet and immediately after that I found myself helplessly vomiting into the basin. My body was making its own protest over maltreatment.

Finally, after washing face and hands in the coldest water I could run, I emerged to join the family for dinner. "Honey girl, you look pale," my mother said with an appraising glance. "Are you all right?" The best I could do was nod.

Daddy served the plates and one look at mine was more than enough. "Excuse me, PLEASE—" and I bolted from the table.

Mother had followed me. "Please, could I just go up and lie down," I begged when my nausea eased. My code demanded silence about what had really happened, so I muttered something about getting too hot and how hard it had been to go back to school. Mother looked a bit unbelieving but tucked me into bed, said she'd come back after dinner, and returned to the table.

Bed had never felt so good, and after my father had come up for prayers and a goodnight kiss, I fell asleep too fast to make any resolutions about what I would do next time if. . .

In the morning I felt fine, a little stiff perhaps, but I was only nine and resilient. If I had been more cautious, it would have been better, because after school the gang was there in full force, each with a friend. "We told 'em what you did yesterday," volunteered one of the boys. "Betcha won't do it again!"

"Darers go first," I remembered to say.

"Scaredy cat! Scaredy cat!" The chant began in full voice. This time I wasn't angry and I didn't run into the barn. I felt trapped, sentenced to public destruction. My steps dragged as I climbed the stairs to the loft. And when I got to the window and looked down, I knew only too well what lay below. No last words came to my lips— they were sealed in despair. I took a deep breath and jumped. . .

"Margaret!" my mother's call was a shriek that I heard just before I hit the ground, and before I could roll over she was there. "Honey girl, honey girl," she murmured as she went rapidly over bones and joints to check me for injuries. "What happened?" The question was addressed to all of us although my audience was rapidly drifting away.

Mother helped me to the house. She put cool washcloths on my head and checked a rapidly swelling ankle and some scrapes on knee and elbow. I was spared the nausea of the day before but had more visible scars to show. It was hard to explain later just what had happened, but when I finally got to "Dare! Dare!" and "Scaredy cat!" my parents exchanged knowing glances and there was some serious talk. I was only too happy to promise NEVER to jump from the hayloft onto the barnyard, ever again.

Bolstered by that parental edict, I told the gang that the barn was off limits except for meetings in the hayloft. No one raised any objections. Adult rulings can be very helpful at times. But proud as I was of my daring and durability, I felt a small bump of caution begin to grow.

We could still use the barnyard for hide-and-seek, and sometimes we tried to hide behind the seventy-five or a hundred large clay sewer pipes stored on end in the far corner of the lot. It was fun to try to walk or crawl over the tops of these pipes, teeter dangerously on the rims, and struggle to keep from falling into the four foot sections. There even came a day when I varied the game with a great idea. Why couldn't I squeeze down inside one of the pipes where I couldn't be seen? Crawling over the front tiers, I found a pipe in the exact middle so that it would be next to impossible to see me unless I stood clear up. I dropped down into the chosen cylinder just as the call came for the search: "Here I come! Ready or not!" Hastily, I scrunched down, chin on knees, rump on heels, back pressed against the brown glazed pipe.

From that secure position, I heard the game go on. Everyone else was caught or shouted triumphantly as he ran home free. They called my name, they shouted, "Allee, allee out's in free!" I decided to stand up, although I didn't want to reveal my choice hiding place. To my surprise, I found that I could not stand; when I tried to straighten my body from its cramped position, my knees pushed against one part of the heavy pipe and my back was forced against another. I was stuck—tightly, absolutely. Frightened, I tried again but only managed to rub some skin off back and knees. Keeping my hiding place a secret seemed a poor idea now. I wanted to be found, knew I needed help. The baked earth smell of the clay around me made my stomach queasy. My shouts were muffled by the pipe around and above me. I could hear my friends, deciding to go home, give up the search. I screamed some more.

Then one of the boys went to the back door and asked if I had made my way stealthily into the house. Alarmed by his tale, Elizabeth called my mother. She called my father. The search was on in earnest. Even my younger brother joined in. And I did my best to guide them as in the old familiar "hot and cold" hiding game. This was no game for me, however, as I fought back tears and tried to save my voice when no one seemed to be in the barnyard. When voices came nearer, I yelled at top strength. And finally my father's voice commanded, "Quiet! I think that was Margaret." Into the sudden silence, I shouted as loud as I could, "Here I am! In the pipes!" Things moved fast from then on. We called back and forth. The boys crawled over the tops of the clay cylinders. One of them saw my waving hand against the dark brown glaze. Will Carr came crawling after him and tried to stand in one pipe next to me and pull me up out of my tight wedge. It was not possible. I thought my arms had been lifted out of their sockets.

The disc of sky that I could see from my circular prison grew darker. The calls of neighborhood men and boys who had come to join in the rescue echoed among the pipes. My head ached. My stomach churned. I heard talk of calling the fire department, but the immediate problem lay in moving the massive pipes aside in order to gain enough room to lay my prison down and work at releasing me feet first. Estimating the shortest way in, the mob began to move pipes until they had cleared a pathway to my now hateful hiding place. Telling me to cushion my head with my arms, my father, Will Carr, and two others raised one side of my clay cage and lowered it gently to the ground. There it lay with me still in it until they gave me some vaseline that Mother had brought from the house and told me to smear it in around my trapped knees. Then, one at a time, very tenderly, Mother and Daddy began to move my legs. "More vaseline, honey, more vaseline. Use it all." And finally one leg came free. That, of course, released me because the other leg had room to move and I could be pulled out straight, by my feet. It was somewhat undignified, but I was out!

The stable yard was declared out of bounds for two months after that and then came winter, and by the time spring had brought us all outside again, I was ready for skating and cycling and swinging. The boys were talking baseball and marbles. We began to go our separate ways.

## The Bees

My father was an amateur bee-keeper, more genuinely interested in the social structure of the hive than
in the tending of the bees. The big volume of
Maeterlinck's *The Bee* was often spread out for us to
marvel over and talk about. Jimmie and I loved to see
Daddy dress for his duties in a long linen duster, gloves
that stretched above the elbow and held themselves up
with tight elastics, and a wide-brimmed hat shrouded in
a heavy veil. He didn't look like our father then but like
some foreign traveler to whom any adventure might
happen.

Sometimes the bees provided high drama when rival
queens forced a swarm to leave the hive and thunder out
in a black, hissing cloud to search for a new home. One
June midday, Daddy hurried home from the campus on
a quick trip between graduation ceremonies and the
trustees' luncheon to pick up a forgotten briefcase. He
found a swarm forming. He was still in his billowing
academic robes—heavy silk faille, black velvet, the beautiful blue philosophy hood hanging over his shoulders.
Pressed for time, he snatched up his "bee-gun," which
blew a sulphorous cloud into the flying insects, exchanged gold-tasseled mortar board for bee hat and veil,
and assumed that his black gown would replace the
usual duster. Running out beyond the servants' house,
he disappeared into the corn stalks and then, almost at
once, reappeared, racing at full speed, robes floating behind him as he cried, "Edna! Edna! Get the hose!"

My mother, dressed in her summer best, dashed out
to meet him and saw that the swarm of bees had chosen
him for their target, clinging to his garments, crawling
into any opening, stinging in their frenzy. Men have
been killed in just this way.

I stood aghast. Mother played the full force of the water on my father as he turned and turned to expose every surface to the spray. His hat was washed off and hung down his back over the sagging blue hood, held only by the elastic hem of the bee veil. The corded silk proved to be surprisingly waterproof but eventually hung about him like a funereal shower curtain. His suit, of course, was drenched. Nothing in Maeterlinck had prepared me for this.

As soon as he could, Daddy dodged into the shelter of the broad screened porch and Mother helped him take off his water-soaked clothes. Will Carr, our yard man, stood by to swat the occasional bee that had survived and then took robe and suit and shirt outside to hang on the line. Jimmie and I were as dazed to see our father trouserless in loose-fitting BVD's as we had been by the excitement of the bees' attack. The sight of a score or more of the villains still hanging from his body by their stingers was frightening. Mother pulled them off, one by one, crooning softly, "Oh, Ralph, dearest, you will be all right!"

Elizabeth, our hired girl, had been busy making a poultice of Arm and Hammer baking soda and water. By the time Dr. Ellis arrived, Daddy was lying on a couch on the porch while Mother plastered his stings. No trustees' luncheon for them that day. Daddy was lucky, as Dr. Ellis said, to get off with his life.

## Go Tell It on the Mountain

Daddy always talked a lot with us when we went to a different church. It wasn't a spectacle, he said, it was just a different means of worship. Men were so varied one from another, he went on, that it seemed necessary for them to choose different paths to God and even to call Him by different names. Growing up in the South post World War I, where it had been patriotic to Save the World for Democracy and was considered by many people equally heroic for the Klan to keep the country pure through systematic harassment of blacks, Catholics, and Jews, I could easily have reached adulthood believing that one true religion—preferably Protestant, white and mainly middleclass—was the only permissible faith. Daddy's insatiable curiosity, his interest and belief in all mankind saved me from that.

In the small college town where I grew up in the Ozarks, there were only about eight different faiths represented officially in perhaps twelve different churches. We were the only family in town who had attended services in each one, and I sometimes had to defend this kind of visiting around to my friends at school. "How come you all were at our church last Sunday," Blanche Mock asked, "you aiming to be a Baptist?"

Blanche was the friend who had been lost with me from the Girl Scout hike the summer before. Our friendship had barely survived the seven or eight hours of wandering and the even division of four boxes of Campfire marshmallows and two dozen bananas—our only food for the day—meant to be shared among the two troops who were on the excursion. After we were found and returned home, Blanche had been sick for a couple of days and carried a real grudge toward me for staying well.

She went with her family to the First Baptist Church on College Avenue. It looked like a giant popover done in creamy yellow stucco with a round amber dome. Wonder of wonders, it had a small pool right in front of the altar. It wasn't for swimming or bathing, my father explained, but for something called immersion that you did with your clothes on. He told us further that this kind of baptism was what gave Baptists their name, and that they were following the example of John the Baptist in this way of declaring their faith.

To conceal my envy of a church that had a baptismal font, as Daddy called it, I tried to tell Blanche all about what he had said. "Humph," she sniffed, "I'll just bet that sprinkling won't get you near as close to heaven as a good dunking." And then she told me about going down to the White River in the summer with her cousins for a real big baptism. "The preacher stood right out in the river and Deacon Smithers helped and everybody wore white robes." It sounded wonderfully dramatic to me at about eleven, and I made a mental note to ask Daddy why we had to keep on being Presbyterians.

Perhaps, I thought, it was because the United Presbyterian Church was on Dickson Street, the closest church to our house. It was red brick with a stylish corner entrance of gleaming marble and stood right across the street from the big Fayetteville Laundry—that is, until the laundry burned down one Saturday night, the biggest fire I had ever seen and not even a block away. The firemen shouted at each other and poured floods of water from their massive hoses, but you could see the supporting timbers stand out like a skeleton against the red flames until the roof fell down and covered everything in a monstrous bonfire. Mother had to buy new sheets and towels and shirts for Daddy after that fire.

Next morning as we peered over the black ruins and watched the firemen play their hoses over the embers, I thought the whole affair had given a much-needed touch of drama to the severe service at the Presbyterian church. Even our hymns were melancholy, except for Easter and Christmas. When the choir stood erect in their black robes and sang, "Praise ye the Lord, the Almighty, the King of creation," majestically as the Hymnal directed, it conveyed no joy. Indeed, it sounded instructive, imperative. "Abide With Me," started out all right but before long "Change and decay in all around I see" turned up and made me shiver. I particularly dreaded,"When death's cold sullen stream shall o'er me roll." My father had his hands full as he directed me toward "What a friend we have in Jesus," and the rousing "Stand up, stand up for Jesus, ye soldiers of the Cross." Fortunately, "Onward, Christian Soldiers" was sung often enough to make me happy.

Happy, that is, until I heard my father's fine tenor rise up out of the congregational melange and take up a life of its own. That he refused to go meekly along with the melody, as I did of necessity, was a source of deep embarrassment to me, but I was never able to persuade him to change. Daddy liked to sing! It seemed to me some kind of showing off—a thing my father never did.

The sermons were long and intellectual, earnestly trying to teach us something. Since it was not considered proper to ask questions then, I soon learned not to listen and used the time to good advantage, daydreaming. After church the sermons were usually discussed anyway, and I could ask questions freely. My father told me a little about John Calvin and Calvinism. It sounded dire to me. Then he went on to the strictness of his own childhood with Grandma and Grandpa. Playing, even quietly, was forbidden as was reading, other than the Bible. His parents did permit the small boy to re-read his Sunday School papers and prick the open letters, o, a, e, q, etc., with a pin. This small pleasure was almost impossible for me to comprehend. I was grateful for our tradition of napping or reading in the afternoons following Sunday dinner at noon, and always having hot chocolate and frequently Welsh rarebit or creamed chipped beef for Sunday supper when Elizabeth, our hired girl, was not there.

The Lord's Supper at Communion was infrequently observed at our church, but it came at regular intervals—once a month as I remember. I looked forward to the silver plates of crackers and the doubledeck servers of grape juice, and I felt immensely grown-up, if hardly sanctified, when I chose my tiny glass (the fullest one within reach), drained it, and set the emptied glass neatly in the bracket provided on the back of the pew in front. Presbyterians had to make the most of what rituals they had not managed to eliminate!

Mother and Daddy both managed, somehow, to soften the doctrine of pre-destination and fore-ordination for me and implant a more latter-day emphasis on the universal love of God. There was no talk of fire and brimstone in our home, and the natural depravity of man was viewed with compassion rather than accusation. My father was always an elder in the church, and I well remember his supportive attitude when at age eleven I appeared before the Session to affirm my decision to become a member of the church.

The decision had not been made lightly. Our visits to different churches had had a powerful influence on me, and since Daddy welcomed questions, I could ask about whatever I liked. He taught classes at the university in the psychology and philosophy of religion and was a great source of information about the differences between religion and theology, faith and ritual, intellectual thinking about God and worship—none of which was dispensed in these terms. He believed wholeheartedly in man's need for a higher power and was truly open to discovery of the many ways man had worked out to serve that need. Dogma played a very minor role in his thinking. In the South of that period, my parents managed to give us a vividly ecumenical experience long before such liberalism was common or fashionable.

A good many of my friends attended the Methodist church, just a block up Dickson Street from ours. It, too, was red brick and white stone, but it seemed to me to house a much more lively observance of Christianity than did the Presbyterian service. Their hymn book contained some of the music I was used to hearing, but many of the tunes were rhythmically appealing, marches or dancelike—as when the congregation swung into, "Yield not to temptation for yielding is sin," and I wanted to clap and twirl. Their Epworth League meetings, too, were much more fun than the rather somber youth meetings at our church. I was pleased that my parents let me go along with Ruth and Marguerite and Maxine to taste the fruits of Methodism. I was very tempted to become a Methodist. Daddy explained, however, that the Methodist ban on dancing was at strange variance with their driving church music. Perhaps, since I liked to dance so much, I'd better wait a while before I declared myself.

The real dancers in town were the Episcopalians. They played cards, too, and many of Fayetteville's social leaders were members of that church. High Church or Low Church was a question that I had heard asked about them and found no meaning for such a query since there was only one small church building, gray stone and of medium height. My father explained the difference in terms of ritual rather than architecture and spoke of the separation of the Protestant from the Catholic church. Fayetteville's congregation chose to be High Church. I liked the robed priest and greatly favored going up to the rail for communion at each service. It carried more devotional meaning for me than our occasional party-like serving of grape juice. Their music was more chant-like but no more lively than ours;

but the Episcopalians seemed very dressy, perhaps the most worldly and sophisticated church-goers in town.

Their derivation from the Catholic church was easy for me to see, aided by the inescapable similarities in ritual. The Catholic chapel in Fayetteville was a very small, rather obscure building set back under mammoth magnolia trees. I found the mysteries of the mass, always said in Latin at that time, truly puzzling, and I always had many questions to ask at home after we attended the service. I loved the drama of the mass, thrilled to the candles and incense, admired the vestments of the priest, and greatly favored all the physical activity involved: kneeling to pray, standing to sing or chant, and sitting only a meager portion of the time to listen and learn from the homily. Daddy explained that for reasons I did not understand we were not welcome to join the line for communion. My father and the Catholic priest of many years standing were good friends, and their never-ending discussions ranged widely from religion to secular matters. Both men were great storytellers.

It was partly due to Father Denis's friendship, I am sure, that Daddy was able to provide a home for ten or twelve teaching nuns who wanted to come up to the university summer session, which my father directed. In one of his roles as a high school inspector, he had been very active in encouraging the parochial schools in Arkansas to bring their curricula, plants, and faculties up to accreditation. Working with the Catholic hierarchy, he had won approval for a limited number of sisters from various downstate schools to come up to the campus during the summer session for graduate studies. Housing, however, presented a problem. The nuns must live together, their privacy protected in some way. The dormitories were not approved, no boarding house was large enough. Finally, a large home diagonally across the street from our house and recently left empty by the owner's death was secured and made ready for the black-robed visitors. They moved in like a flock of happy blackbirds, studied in the porch swings, and practiced their tennis strokes on the front lawn, holding their habits out of the way as they ran.

The Klan was very active in Arkansas then, and some of my friends whose fathers were Ku Klux members prophesied trouble for my father as the result of his daring sponsorship of the nuns' residence, but he paid little attention to the phone calls, some threatening, some approving, that he received about his plan. Mother called on the sisters, taking me along and leaving the appropriate number of cards: one for each nun. She hospitably invited them in for tea at a later date. How surprised I was when they laughed and giggled over the many strange situations they found themselves in at summer school! They were real people. I began to question the ugly tales I had been told by my peers about guns buried under the cathedrals for each Catholic baby born. A religious uprising armed in this way seemed very unlikely from these interesting women or Father Denis, himself. Once more, I would have to ask Daddy.

Visits to the Christian church, now called the Church of Christ, seemed to me very like the Methodist and Baptist services, any one of which was more lively than the Presbyterian pattern and none as colorful or dramatic as the Episcopal or Catholic mass. The Church of Christ Scientist struck me as being more like an elaborate business meeting or a lecture than a religious observance. We went home loaded with literature which I knew my father would read. It was too much like school for me. In my rather limited view, my grandfather, a physician, took precedence over Mary Baker Eddy, and there was little my father could do to explain away my prejudice. When we visited Grandma and

Grandpa in Moran, religion was kept neatly in place in the white steepled Presbyterian church across from Grandpa's office, and science and health (in lower case letters) were attended to in his medical chambers. It was impossible for me to imagine any other alignment.

Fayetteville had no Jewish synagogue, and the only person that I can ever remember hearing identified as a Jew was another friend of Daddy's, Mr. Silverman, the jeweler. He was a small, neat man, exquisitely courteous—even to children—and I thought it marvelous that his name matched his profession. It was on trips away from Fayetteville that we were first able to visit a Jewish service as a family. As I remember, we attended the service in Chicago with a friend of Daddy's from Scott, Foresman and Company. I was most impressed by the canopy and listened with delight to the rich voice of the cantor.

In Vancouver, British Columbia, we had the memorable experience of attending the service in a Sikh temple. I had been immensely impressed with the many tall, bearded men in formal turbans on the city streets and felt for the first time a little shy about being at a strange church. Leaving my shoes on the wide veranda and finding that Mother and I would sit on the floor in a different part of the big room from my father and Jimmie made me even more unsettled. But then I became aware of a wonderfully colorful happening that captured my full attention: in front of what I would have identified as the altar was an inclined plane, at least four by six feet in size, covered with green brocade. Around it on the floor was a sort of gutter about a foot wide. And my astonished eyes saw Sikh after Sikh come in, dip his head toward the green surface, and throw his offering directly on it! It made a splendid show; the bills fluttered to the floor like long leaves, the coins bounced and ricocheted and finally rolled into the gutter, where they shone in the candlelight. What a great way to make people happy about their giving! Presbyterianism had nothing to equal this.

I was learning, I think, that each service we attended had a special quality of its own, and by the reach of my imagination I could project my curiosity and wonder into the multitude of churches, temples, mosques, tabernacles, cathedrals, and shrines I might never see. This was my father's enduring legacy to me.

The only service available that we didn't visit as a family was that of the Holy Rollers, a splinter Evangelical sect, that held summer camp meetings in a grove near the river. Where they met in the winter, I never knew. Hidden in the woods with friends, all of us there without parental sanction, I watched with fascination and shock the, to me, hysterical observances favored and promoted by a series of shouting preachers of hell, damnation and, hopefully (if one repented in time), salvation. We saw people possessed by the spirit jump and run and fall and roll, scream "Hallelujah! Praise the Lord!," speak in tongues, embrace relatives and strangers until they subsided in quivering huddles of flesh or were led away by family members. This was sideshow stuff, indeed, and I finally had to confess my going to Daddy and ask why my compulsion to watch was so colored with fear and repugnance. He heard me out, asked a few quiet questions, and pointed out that I had not gone as a potential worshipper but as a Peeping Tom. Their excesses, he said, were not compatible with the way he personally felt about worship but possibly filled their need. "I prefer to know what I'm doing when I serve my God," he added.

The church I most enjoyed attending—partly, I'll admit, because of my friends' mixture of awe and revulsion when they heard we had been there—was the AME Zion church in Tin Cup, the black community in

Fayetteville. So far as I know, we were the only white family in town to go to their services, but many of our good friends were there: Will Carr, our yard man; Lily, our laundress; the shoeshine man from the Washington Hotel; the doorman at the bank, and others we saw regularly around town. Mother always dressed carefully for church and took special pains to see that our appearance, as well as hers, was in order when we visited other churches. For our worship at the AME Zion church, she saw to it that we were truly at our best in both dress and behavior. Appearing to our black friends in this way could have been awkward at best, and Mother felt as deeply as Daddy that we were stretching the privilege of friendship. She would not have shamed them by being careless in any way. After the startled stiffness of our first visit, everyone was warm and welcoming. They all "made over" Jimmie and me, and they sang like the proverbial angels.

The reason I loved it so was the music. They worshipped joyfully and fearfully, sadly, and with determination. When the choir lined out, "I couldn't hear nobody pray," and the deep basses answered, "No," only to hear the reaffirmation, "I couldn't hear nobody pray," before the soloist wailed in anguish, "Away down yonder by myself," I was close to tears and ready to join in with the final, "And I couldn't hear nobody pray." It made me know what utter desolation could be like.

I was ready for the resolute struggle of "Go Down, Moses," the sublime confidence of "I Know the Lord's Laid His Hands on Me," the puzzle of "Wheel in a Wheel," and the happy singalong of "Ring Them Charming Bells." And when "Little David Play on Your Harp" pealed forth, Daddy's tenor sounded just right. My father loved the spirituals even more than I did, and we had records of the Fisk Jubilee Singers to listen to and sing with at home and a copy of the National Jubilee

Melodies to sound out on the piano. At Christmas time, the joy of "Go Tell It on the Mountain" was as much part of the glorious good news as "Adeste Fidelis."

My father's personal faith was deep, a staunch belief that carried his questioning mind far afield and home again. When my love brought me to marriage with a Catholic husband, my parents' hearts held only joy for our ecumenical venture. And it seemed abundantly fitting that the last words my father spoke in this world were, "I want to pray."

## The Thunderstorm

*Mama didn't go by what other people thought.*
*She said, "Put on your bathing suit*
*or an old shift. Stay away from the trees."*
*My suit was too hard to pull on—tight wool knit*
*over hot sticky skin. The shift was easy.*
*Faded blue, it stood away from my sticky heat.*
*I tried to tie up my hair but there wasn't time.*
*I had to get back outside. Something*
*might happen.*

*I ran onto the lawn, flying over*
*the smooth cistern top, around a honeysuckle*
*screen, out from under the fountain-like elm.*
*The grass showed a shocking green in the*
*mustard*
*light.*

*Never had I been so hot.*
*The sky, a sealed dome, closed over me,*
*a bell jar holding formal, solid air.*
*Nothing moved, nothing even breathed.*
*The catalpa leaves we used for dolls'*
*umbrellas were motionless. From the*
*tall elm, my bag swing was a fifteen*
*foot plumb-bob, stiff on its rope.*

*There I stood, a thin statue*
*left over from a forgotten game. Slowly*
*my arms stretched out and up, I rose*
*on tiptoe, I drew my breath in,*
                            *in,*
                    *in.*
*I could feel my ribs ache.*

*And then it happened—the sky dome*
*split with a bolt of green fire and its*
*cracking could be heard like God's own*
*whip across the clouds. I danced in*
*the deluge, blown with the leaves that*
*swirled around me. My long curls*
*hung sodden seaweed-brown about my*
*shoulders. My shift, nearly ripped off*
*by the first blast, clung to my cooling*
*body, a second skin. Released from the*
*prison of waiting, my howl*
*joined the scream of the wind.*

## Brother/Sister

Leaving a charmed infancy behind him, Jimmie grew into a strangely threatened boyhood, prone to every illness or infection circulating at the time. My hard heart felt little sympathy for his flushed fevers, his racking coughs. Instead, I was consumed with envy over the attention he received. We had many of the same childhood diseases, brought them home to one another from friends and classmates, but what a difference! Whooping cough was a six-week convulsive disaster for him; I barely produced a feeble cough or two. Red measles were hardly visible on my dark skin, his blondness showed the insult of a consuming eruption, and he had the further effrontery to carry on into pneumonia. I didn't even bother to have the chicken-pox that was so painful for him. Occasionally I realized how privileged my good health made me, but more often I yearned after the special concern and nursing he needed.

Jimmie was a surprisingly good-natured child, considering his frequent bouts with illness, and in his curiosity about how things worked and the minutiae of their makeup earned the well-deserved reputation among family friends of being "the observant one." Although I can't remember Mother or Daddy ever using the hated phrase, I can still hear myself saying crossly, "I look at what I want to!" Books did not enchant him, I noticed—meanly.

I must have made a horrid older sister, and Jimmie retaliated by being the classic younger brother tease. He was especially fond of mocking my serious-minded efforts to shine as the senior child in the family. Of course, I never felt that he was properly punished for tormenting me and was quick to point out such deficiencies to my long-suffering parents. They were such fair-minded people, I thought, how could they fall into such blatant favoritism?

On one memorable year, the Fourth of July fell on Sunday and we were forbidden any fireworks until the following day; even the official town celebration was postponed until what was to be that year the Glorious Fifth. Most distressing of all was the dictum that the cannon was not to be fired. My brother's treasure, the cannon—less than my father's hand in length—was a family heirloom, made, the legend went, from metal melted down from a Revolutionary War fire-piece that had burst in battle. It had been my father's, James Ralph Jewell, as only son of his father, James Erastus Jewell, as eldest son of James Jewell, and so on back to Colonial times. Each year it made its ceremonial appearance to be stuffed with gunpowder and wadding, a fuse laid to it, and fired off using a proper-sized pebble or marble in place of a cannon ball. Daddy said quietly, "I know it's hard, Jimmie. I'll just put the cannon away until tomorrow," and disappeared upstairs with the miniature fire-piece in his hand.

At thirteen, I was old enough to know when the die was cast; nothing exciting was going to happen until tomorrow. I settled down with a book and was soon lost to the disappointing real world. Mother was deep in her ritual afternoon nap. Daddy was at his desk. Mrs. Donnelly, our cook, was probably in her room. But Jimmie and his nine-year-old friends intended to salvage what they could of Independence Day and put their frustration to work in unexpected ways.

He still had his store of gunpowder, purchased with Daddy for the eventual loading and firing of the antique memento and kept in a tight oval Postum tin against accidental ignition. Surely that ammunition could be put to good use. So Jimmie and his friends dug a deep, narrow hole, "to be safe," and poured quite a charge of gunpowder into its bottom. Then they carefully laid a long, perhaps eighteen inch fuse for some distance—again to be safe. All the boys crowded at the end of the fuse as it was lit. The fuse crackled slowly toward the hole for what must have seemed an eternity. It burned over the edge and down into the hole. The boys waited. . .and waited. No splendid flare. They waited. . .And finally Jimmie went up to see why it had not fired. Just as he bent over, the explosion went off in his face, throwing sandy earth and burning powder in his eyes and hair. Gone were his blond eyelashes, singed stubble replaced his front hair, his fair skin blistered, and he screamed with pain from his scorched eyeballs. Everyone came running. A hurried call went out to Dr. Ellis. Mother put cool boric acid pads over Jimmie's eyes. Daddy got out the car. The boys scattered as if blown by the gunpowder. I was kept running for more water, more cotton, more gauze. Mrs. Donnelly stood keening, her face buried in her apron.

Dr. Ellis shook his head over the damage and said we would have to wait to know how great it had been. Jimmie's skin burns were treated and eased, his hair would grow back as would his eyebrows and lashes, but it was days, perhaps about two weeks, before we learned that his vision would be saved. During that period, even my stony heart was full of prayers for my brother. It had certainly been his most dramatic play for attention, but I could imagine no worse fate than to lose one's sight. I practiced with a folded towel to simulate his bandages— no light, all dark, no sky, no mountains rising against it, no books. The enormity of never being able to read again shook my whole being.

Sad to say, my surprisingly mellow feelings toward him, acquired at such great cost, lasted only until he had recovered and we returned to our normal pattern of tease and taunt. Chasing each other through house and garden was a particular favorite of ours, and we pretended anger even when it was a game, yelling accusations and imprecations as we flew up and down stairs and in and out of doors while Mrs. Donnelly threatened us with every punishment known to God or man. To our parents we said innocently, "but we were only playing," but after Jimmie tore his hand on a door and then, jumping back, suffered a gash in his head from the strike-plate, our running and chasing through the house was banned. The fond hope was that somehow or other we could grow up safely.

BumBum, was our adored baby sister, born when I was eleven and Jimmie seven. That had been the year of the post-World War I flu epidemic, and Mother was sent home from the hospital with her new baby after only a few days, in the hope that they could escape infection. BumBum stayed well but my mother became ill; then Jimmie (who always "had things hard") went rapidly from classic influenza to pneumonia. A bed was made for him in the dining room, and my father and Elizabeth went on twenty-four hour nursing duty with the help of a practical nurse who came in daily. I was isolated in my sunny upstairs bedroom on a diet of blanc mange. This delicacy, which I hated, was brought to the house in a seemingly endless supply by whatever friends were still ambulatory. I was terminally bored and forlorn but in no danger. Daddy stayed well and spent most of his time in our big double parlor which had been turned into a hospital suite: Mother and the baby in one side and Jimmie in the other. Dr. Ellis came in daily, and Elizabeth raced from kitchen to bedside to washtub, keeping things going. I was too sick to help, not sick enough to worry about, and so I got pretty lonely.

But we all survived, and BumBum (who had been christened in the Southern fashion with family names— Keith Coe Jewell) became our absolute joy. She was slightly built but glowing with health, laughed easily, "talked" a great deal in her own infant language and, as she grew older, proved to be agile, curious, and eager for fun.

## *Spelunking*

*I have come to this cave in a cricket of a Model-T
leaving puffs of dust with each hop along the gravel
road that winds through wooded limestone hills.
As we rode we sang Floyd Collins ballads, frightened
ourselves with tales of his unhappy end, lost in the
honeycomb caverns of Kentucky, where
his brother escaped the rock fall. Floyd's
breathy singing failed as rescuers tunneled
toward him. Delicious chills ran down
our backs. It was better than ghost stories.
It could happen to us.*

*I'm proud because I'm a skinny kid, eleven, and other
spelunkers are real geologists from the campus,
led by Dr. Cady, father of my two friends, and
hoping today to add a new cave to their Ozark
explorations. Ruth and Bud and I have our
role, too. That's why we're here.*
                           *Girdled with
thin strong rope, we'll wriggle through crevices only
our leanness will permit. We'll drop
pebbles into the bottomless dark, judge
distance from the echoing sounds.  Far
far below we hear the ripple of running
water—some pebbles fall a long, long
time before there is an answering plink from*

the river underground. We use sparingly the
flashlights tethered to our wrists, their
beams feeble and white against the pitchy
black. We have found rooms, caverns,
palaces this way before.
                              Nothing equals the
mystery, the cold, the blackness of a cave
newly explored. Hands, feet, body become
strangers that are not, cannot be seen.
Eyes open wide, their muscles strain to
focus on nothing. An unexpected breeze
brushes the skin, speaks of channels, passages
hidden in the dark. The scent is mixed.
Damp stone has never seen the sun, water
drips or runs unseen, clay—cool, moist,
slippery—is underfoot.
Breathing is guarded.

> Black is the color of a cave
> its architecture formal. It grows
> slowly, measuring itself in eons,
> free from the disorder of the world
> above. Here a ledge dissolves,
> there a stone icicle becomes a
> pillar—all in due time.
>                              A sigh
> of silence, whispers turn to
> echoes, sink in the marble dark.

Now we'll go back along our tugging rope,
try to remember turns and shallow tunnels,
scrawl grubby maps and
                              suddenly turn cold,
eager as Persephone to join the world above,
feel sun and wind or even rain
in random quick-paced life again.

## Why I Wasn't Playing in the Superbowl

Whenever football hype reaches its peak, I am reminded of the humiliation I suffered at the end of my football career. At my prime, between my eleventh and twelfth birthdays, I was the star running back of my neighborhood team. Thin, wiry, and fleet of foot, I could outrun any boy on the squad and was the only girl on the team. I valued my status and was both proud of it and completely comfortable with the acceptance accorded me. I was tackled just as hard as any of my teammates and did my best to make up in speed what I lacked in strength and weight. Most of the touchdowns, in fact, were mine!

And then one day, coming in from a bruising practice session, I was met at the front door by my mother. She took one long, appraising look at my disheveled state, tangled hair, grass-stained clothes, a blue lump rising on my cheekbone and followed me to my room upstairs "for a talk." That particular term often had ominous overtones and this time was no exception. Mother announced, kindly but in no uncertain manner, that my life on the gridiron had come to an end.

I couldn't believe my ears. We were planning a big game on Friday with our archrivals from over by the cemetery. My team needed me! Mother was unmoved. I was growing up fast, she said, and must expect "certain changes" that would make me "feel less like a boy." I protested that statement with some vehemence—never ever had I felt like a boy. I was just a fast runner! My reticent mother, the most private individual I have ever known, discussed the matter no further. She would, she said, call my friends' mothers and explain her prohibition if I wished, but the decision was final. I said a quick "No!" to that suggestion.

Humiliated and ashamed, I told my teammates the next day about the ruling. Two of them snickered; I didn't know why. And on Friday afternoon, I had to watch my team go down to defeat before I went home and had a good cry.

## Zephania, Haggai, Zecharia, Malachi

The small violet Bible in my hands is faded, the clump of embossed lilies-of-the-valley on the cover has lost its dull gold and gathered a permanent fine gray dust. The binding has split down the fold of the spine. The onionskin pages have yellowed, and there are many dog-ears to help in finding special passages, but only the note pages at the back and the first chapters of *Malachi* have loosened. It looks comfortable, used, and friendly. For years now it has been at my daughter's bedside.

But when I hold it, I am twelve years old and it is a vibrant violet with the delicious smell of a new book. It is early summer, school will soon be out for the long vacation, and my dear grandmother in Kansas has sent me this special gift. It is the first Bible all my own and has a totally different feel from the enormously heavy family Bible with sharp black steel engravings that one must sit on the floor to look at, carefully turning the pages with clean hands. It differs, too, from my parents' limp black leather Bibles with their silken braids of red, green, and yellow to mark the pages. My Bible can be comfortably held because of its stiff board back and, although the print is small, it is well-formed and easily read. It was printed in Philadelphia by A. J. Holman Co. and states on the fly leaf "the text is conformable to that of the edition of 1611, commonly known as the authorized or King James' version." The opening illustration is of a white-bearded man in tunic and cloak, Elijah, carrying a large lantern to light his way down a rocky mountain path, "into the Jordan," the footnote reads. The text is from Psalm 119, "Thy World is a Lamp unto my feet, and a Light unto my Path."

Grandma had written a letter that accompanied my gift. She pointed out that I was certainly old enough to have my own personal Bible and went on to say how much the Book had meant to her. This I knew, because when we visited I frequently saw her seated in the rose-carved rocker, reading from her own copy with its thin gold-edged pages. She was apt with all too pertinent Biblical quotations, and I had heard the tale about her accustomed response to my father's misdeeds as a small boy. Pulling the child up into her lap—in the same rocker, brought from Tennessee—she would trace with his tiny finger the text, "Be sure your sins will find you out." Then she would hug him and hold him there on her lap for a while after laying the heavy Book aside.

Her letter to me continued to say that while no one should be paid to read the Bible ("What a precious privilege that is!"), she would like to reimburse me for the time it would take from other activities—being with friends, skating, reading other books—if I should choose to spend my free summer hours in this way. In fact, she proposed a gift of fifteen dollars for the Old Testament and ten dollars for the New. A total of twenty-five dollars! Such a sum was almost beyond belief. I fear that avarice was in the ascendancy over holy learning as I shared my letter with my parents and announced my determination to read the Book from cover to cover.

"It is a most important book," Daddy volunteered, "but it is very long and parts are hard to read. Are you sure of

what you are pledging?" And Mother added, "Don't try to
read too much at a time, dear. Take frequent breaks."

I nodded, then shook my head and went off to my
room, Bible in hand. Opening to "The first book of Moses,
called Genesis," I read the familiar words, "In the beginning God created the heaven and the earth." It would
be easy, I thought, visualizing frequent encounters with
texts such as this one made familiar through the common practice of roll call at Sunday School, which was
answered by each student with a memorized Bible verse.
After being forbidden the overly frequent repetition of
"Jesus wept," we had been forced into hasty explorations
for other short quotations. I would surely run across old
friendly texts and make a stockpile of new ones, I
thought. Vanity took over as I envisioned my classmates
dazzled and envious when I paraded my learning in
longer, more dramatic verses.

Mother and Daddy were not so ebullient. Each, having read the Bible at different times, knew better than I
what a challenge lay ahead. Although they never ac-
tively discouraged me, they did point out the thickness of
the book, its thin pages, its fine print, the sheer length
(947 pages in the Old Testament, 289 in the New) of the
text. When I asked how I could prove that I had really
read it all, they said that they would like to talk about it
with me as I went along.

And so began the summer when I read the Bible. It
was 1921, my last summer on Dickson Street. I would be
thirteen in October when we moved to Hill Street.

I wrote Grandma of my intentions and continued on
through *Genesis*. It was familiar to me and the
characters were well known: Adam and Eve, Noah—the
Flood and the Ark. Chapter Five detailing "the
generations of Adam" startled me with the stated ages:
Adam, 930 years; Seth, 912 years; Methusaleh, the

legendary 969. I had learned Methusaleh's age from the spiritual,

> *Methusaleh was a witness, Oh my Lord,*
> *He lived nine hundred and ninety-nine*
> *And died and went to heaven*
> *All in a-due time. . .*

When I asked my father about the thirty year discrepancy, I learned something about poetic license. And thirty years in a lifetime of that length didn't really seem to matter that much. The other ages were, however, a surprise. Noah was 500 years old when he "begat Shem, Ham, and Japhet" and they were young men at the time of the Flood. Noah died after 950 years of eventful living. What had happened to the human race? Had we lost our ability to survive? I knew that my own grandparents, both seventy-five at the time, were considered aged. My parents, who were forty-one and forty-three that year, seemed old to me.

While I read quickly, and material such as Chapter 10, which detailed the generations of Noah, could be sped through, questions and interesting bits of information kept popping up. Even Chapter 10 had a word about Nimrod, "the mighty hunter before the Lord." I couldn't go too fast for fear of missing something. The Tower of Babel appeared next, and then came the recorded generations of Shem and Terah which I whizzed through. And, interestingly enough, lives grew shorter. Terah lived a mere 205 years.

Abram and Sarai (Sarah) and Lot and Pharaoh and Sodom and Gomorrah took center stage as I read on, posing further questions. The men "of Sodom were wicked and sinners before the Lord." What had they done? I also puzzled, as have many others, over Hagar and Ishmael. And then when Abram was ninety-nine years old, he was renamed Abraham, father of many nations, by the Lord, and when he was one hundred and his wife ninety, a son, Isaac, was born to them. As if that weren't startling enough, Abraham very nearly killed Isaac and offered him up as a sacrifice. I would never finish reading the Bible, I thought, if it keeps turning up with so many surprises.

Then came Rebecca and her markedly unlike twin sons, Jacob and Esau, who grew up in such distrust of one another that they behaved very strangely indeed. I found Jacob hard to like because of the way he and his mother tricked Isaac into blessing him instead of Esau. And even after he worked so many years to get Rachel, his wife, and then had so many children with Leah, her older sister, whom he had to marry first before Rachel had Joseph, I felt that Jacob was one to watch closely.

But in *Genesis* I did come upon the familiar and comforting blessing, "The Lord watch between me and thee, when we are absent one from another," that was often repeated at the close of our church service and always when we told our grandparents goodbye after a visit.

Joseph's prophetic dreams and his life after being sold into Egypt, the famine and his treatment of his older brothers, his trickery with the silver cup to keep Benjamin with him, and finally his reunion with Jacob, his father, were so exciting to me that I waded through many pages of rather confusing relationships. But Jacob finally died, and his devoted son, Joseph, took the body back to the land of Canaan, and then Joseph died at a mere 110 and I had finished *Genesis*.

*Exodus* kept up the pace set by *Genesis* with Moses and the bulrushes and his much later journey up to the mountain of God and the burning bush and his commission to deliver Israel. A rod that turns into a serpent is magical stuff, and a river that turned into blood was as fearsome to me as it had been to the Egyptians. Again, I was helped by the spirituals I had heard so often, "Go down, Moses, way down in Egypt's land. Tell Old Pharaoh, Let my people go." But it was not until the Passover that Moses was commanded to lead his people to the Promised Land. And he did just that. Through the Red Sea they went as it parted before them and celebrated their freedom with songs and dancing. In the long journey that followed, the children of Israel complained at their hardships for forty years and were nourished on manna (which sounded like the communion wafers at our church) and were finally given the Ten Commandments. I had long since memorized those commandments and was completely convinced that they were chiseled out of two large stone tablets that Moses carried down the mountain, one in each arm. I had seen pictures of that very scene.

The punishments decreed sounded pretty brutal to me: "Life for life, eye for eye, tooth for tooth, hand for hand, foot for foot." More laws and ordinances followed, and then came the intriguing instructions about how to make an ark and a tabernacle and even how to weave the curtains for the tabernacle. They sounded gorgeous— blue and purple and scarlet, with cherubims. Burnt offerings were described and how to make incense and holy annointing oil. Moses and Aaron, his brother, must have been busy men. Moses, especially, spent a great deal of time with God, getting all the instructions straight. And when the tabernacle was completed, a cloud descended on it and, as the children of Israel continued their journey, "the cloud of the Lord was upon the tabernacle by day and the fire was on it by night," and I had finished *Exodus.*

I found a certain morbid pleasure in Chapter 13 of *Leviticus* as I read the symptoms of leprosy, examining myself as carefully as possible to make sure that I was not unclean. Remembrance of the returned missionary who had talked to our Sunday School class and given a gruesomely vivid account of her term of duty in a leper's colony in India checked with the instructions given Moses and Aaron. I winced as memory of the pain I had felt when I tested the white spot that I fancied stood out on my left hand with boiling water to see if I could feel it. I could—and did! My father's dismay over my gullibility tempered his concern over my scalded hand. "Margaret!" he shook his head. "Why didn't you talk about it with us?" His arm was tight around my shoulders. Cold water ran over my burning hand.

Reading *Leviticus* raised many questions, since there were laws about things I had never heard of like "issues" and "lusts" and "carnal." "Nakedness" I understood, but a whole chapter about it! Mother tended toward deep embarrassment when I tried to clear away my ignorance; Daddy was unembarrassed but a little less than forthright with my probing. The big dictionary on its stand in the library defined terms in such a way as to confuse me further. There were references such as, "Thou shalt not let any of thy seed pass through the fire to Molech" that seemed almost to demand medical knowledge. "Seed?" They had just been going on and on about nakedness and lying down with people. Perhaps I should make a list for Grandpa, a physician. I started such a list but somehow the time never seemed right for discussion, either by mail or in person. Bible reading had its unexpected problems.

The census taking in *Numbers* was quite a relief after the multiple commandments in *Leviticus*, and I sailed through the Levites and the Nazarites and grieved over Miriam's leprosy. It was that deadly whiteness, apparently, that showed the fatal sign. A lot of laws also came to light in *Numbers*, and if it hadn't been for Balaam and his ass I might have given up my project

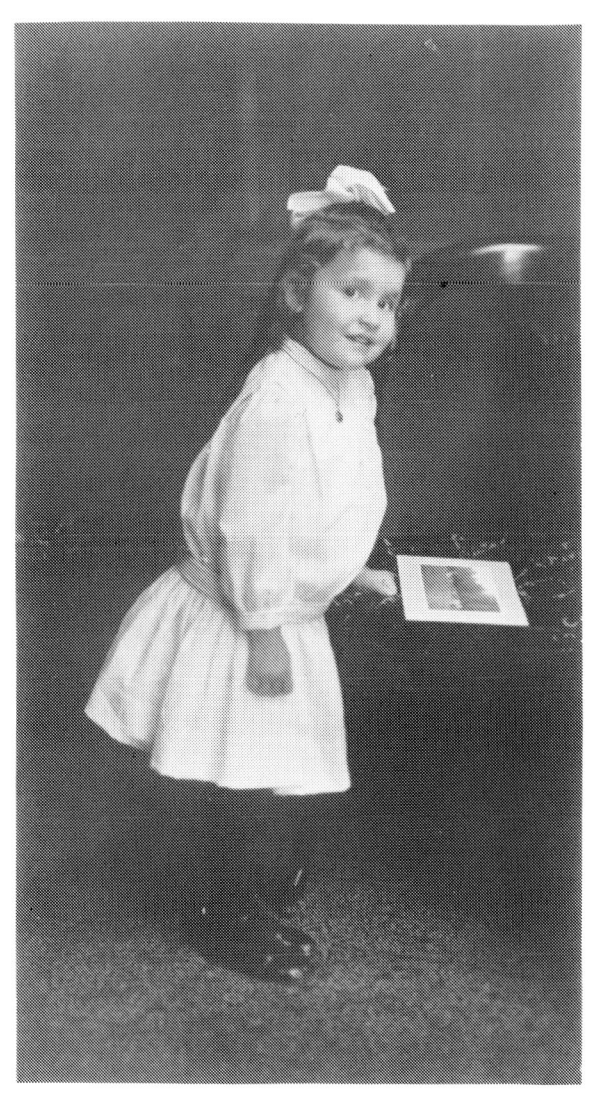

Margaret Elaine Jewell
1912

Mother and Margaret

Green Mountain Falls
Summer of 1912

Daddy and Margaret

Mother, Jimmie, and Margaret
1913

"Home Again!"—Margaret
Autumn 1912

Margaret and Jimmie
1916

The Five of Us
1920

Reading, always reading—1923

In high school—1921

entirely. It is a fearsome thing to attempt to read the
Bible straight through from cover to cover—which was
my plan. When my parents suggested reading the New
Testament first or selecting certain Psalms, I was offended and stubborn. When you read a book, I said, you
open it and read it. You don't skip around from place to
place.

And so I struggled on through *Deuteronomy*—
Joshua and the walls of Jericho, *Judges* with Samson
and Delilah and came upon the beautiful story of *Ruth*—
such a short chapter! I wanted more. *First* and *Second
Samuel* nourished my need for narrative, and I tried
hard, as I had found I must, to keep everyone straight.
Spirituals again rang in my ears, "Little David, play on
your harp—Hallelu—Hallelu—" and how I wished that
I could have seen David "leaping and dancing before the
Lord." How could Saul's daughter—or anyone else, for
that matter—have despised him "in her heart?"

Eventually, David "smote the Philistines and subdued
them" and went on to a severe misunderstanding with
God and misuse of power. And I went on to Bathsheba
and Solomon and the Queen of Sheba and the building of
the temple. It was heady stuff, often misunderstood and
often hastily, thoughtlessly read. I had invented my own
technique for speed reading. My eyes learned to light on
familiar names—Elijah and his chariot of fire, Elisha,
the hairy one, and on words I associated with joy or disaster. "Leprosy" appeared over and over. My skin
crawled at the thought.

After more census records in *Chronicles*, Saul and
David appeared and the story telling was on again.
Colored photographs of "Jericho as it is today," in which
I could see no hint of or place for a well, and a "Shepherd
pasturing his flock"—fat grazing sheep, both black and
white I was happy to see—enlivened these pages, and by
the time I had finished *Second Chronicles*, I had

reached page 520. *Ezra*—more records and a strange passage about strange marriages. *Nehemiah* was short and heavy with unfamiliar names but at last I came to *Esther* and her triumph.

As I ploughed through one thin page after another, an Ozark summer glorified God outside. The skies were a deep, bright blue adorned with mounds of cumulus clouds. Heat mounted into the blaze of noontime, frequent thunderstorms broke that heat with sharp spikes of lightning. Thunder rolls sounded a pounding bass. Evenings tended to be cool, but there was little need for a sweater. Gardens were lavish with their fragrance and color. Tuberoses drooped in the hot air; four o'clock pods curled round your finger when touched. I paid little attention to all this except when I was literally chased out of the house by my mother "to get a breath of fresh air."

Most of the time I lay on my stomach in the library, where I would trade off my little violet Bible for the big print of the family Bible, or in my room propped with pillows, facing the tall wardrobe which served as a closet and held all my clothes. But my favorite place to read was on my deep feather bed on the sleeping porch, a step down from my room. The screen was brushed by the green branches of a large maple. There were squirrels and birds living in that tree. A small white owl had his nest there and kept serene watch over me as I read. Looking across the yard, I could see the outside stairway mounting to my playhouse. I yearned to go there, but I was getting a bit too old for such play, I thought. I was reading the Bible.

Job's sorrows and tribulations brought copious tears. How unfair can life be, I asked over and over, as he did, and rejoiced in his final days of peace. *The Book of Psalms* came as a real blessing, and I reveled in its variety. The directness of its address to the ear of God reminded me of my grandmother and her prayer closet. I could fairly hear her as she demanded, "Hear me when I call, O God of my righteousness," or, "Preserve me, O God, for in thee do I put my trust." I marked with a soft pencil passages that especially spoke to me. I wonder now what prompted, "My God, my God, why hast thou forsaken me?" to be so marked and am relieved to see shortly after a circle around, "Blessed is he whose transgression is forgiven, whose sin is covered." My apparent relief found voice in "Rejoice in the Lord," and, "O clap your hands, all ye people." My twelve-year-old heart seemed to have found more than peace.

*Proverbs* laid out for my instruction rules, regulations, and aphorisms galore. I had to smile when I read, "A soft answer turneth away wrath: but grievous words stir up anger." That seemed to sum up Southern speech and manners for me—how often had I been cautioned about that very thing!

And so it went. In almost every book I happened onto passages familiar to me at that time, although I frequently felt myself slogging through dry records, historical minutiae, names I would forget even as I read them. *Ecclesiastes'* moving testimony, "To everything there is a season," prepared me in a way for the passion of *Solomon*, and I began to understand why it was called a *Song*. To hear my father read from this book as he glanced over my head to my mother was a revelation of love for which I was unprepared but eager.

I was not mature enough yet for *Isaiah* or for many of the prophets and saw them as rather self-important elderly men with long beards and flowing robes. How do we know what they looked like, I began to wonder. It helped that the small pages carried headings that told what the texts were about—sort of a Cliff's Notes before their time. To see "The Jews reproved" or "God's great mercy toward Judah" gave me a necessary clue to the use of metaphors of harlotry and whoredom, not common words to me. The "big" vocabulary of my early childhood was getting bigger.

The profound severity of the Old Testament Jehovah was overwhelming to me at times, and it took lots of reassurance from my parents to keep me from panic. I was relieved and glad to get through *Jeremiah* and his *Lamentations*, which, fortunately for me, were so much shorter than Job's sad story. And when I reached *Ezekiel*, I was in the melodious land of spirituals again.

> *'Zekiel saw the wheel of time*
> *Every spoke was human kind—*
> *Big wheel run by faith*
> *Little wheel run by the grace of God—*
> *Wheel in the middle of a wheel—*

I was beginning to have some faint idea of the fearful and wonderful interlocking of men, past and present, and their views of God and the world. The ability of the prophets to live between the terrible power of God and the human frailties of their people was awesome to me.

*Daniel* appeared like an old friend and he, too, had been celebrated in song, "Daniel Saw the Stone," though not so popularly as David and his harp. And now it was downhill for the Old Testament, in my view. After *Hosea* came a litany of names which could be (and were) repeated like doggerel: *Joel, Amos, Obadiah/Jonah, Micah, Nahum/Habbakuk/Zephania, Haggai, Zecharia, Malachi.* I put myself to sleep at night saying them over and over, and almost before I could believe it, I had finished reading the Old Testament!

The summer seemed sweeter to me now. Swinging high into the trees had been a glorious respite when I needed to stop reading and live for a while; now it had the triumph of victory about it. I knew that I could finish the New Testament; it was a story that I had always known so well. And it did not frighten me. Beginning with the Four Gospels, it told in the words of four men who had known him the story of Jesus. He had been a baby, as had all of us. (I didn't think of him with a capital "H") My little sister was not yet two—babies were very real to me that summer. And he grew out of infancy into boyhood (much more blessed and full of wisdom than my brother, however) and he became a man full of comfort and blessing. He seemed to believe in goodness rather than punishment, and he was always taking the part of people who needed him. I was very happy with *Matthew, Mark, Luke*, and *John*. It didn't bother me at all that they told different versions of the same story. After all, they were four very different men, and maybe they had been assigned various parts of the story. It did puzzle me that Mark would choose to write about Christ's death rather than his birth. My father helped make the four men come alive for me as he did with the parables and the miracles. Daddy told me that Luke was a doctor like Grandpa. I wondered if Luke looked like Grandpa or like Dr. Ellis. I liked the way he told about Jesus eating bread and fish and honey after he rose from the tomb. I wrote Grandma how happy I was with her suggested reading.

John seemed to have a great feeling for light and spoke of it often and of blindness. To him, Christ was a Word, Life, Light, a Door, a Shepherd. John was the one who most often wrote down Christ's own words.

After reading the Gospels, it was easy for me to understand why the Apostles had to do what they did in trying to spread the Word and why their *Acts* had to be recorded. It was like an adventure story, or many stories, and I kept wondering what would happen next. A lot happened—from Saul/Paul's conversion on the road to Damascus to his journeys and letters as an apostle to Rome, to Corinth, to Galatia, to Phillipi, to Colossae, to Thessalonia. Those letters were written from Athens,

Rome, Corinth, Philippi by different scribes from Paul's dictation. What a traveler, I thought.

When *Timothy* began his mission, Paul wrote him two careful letters of instruction. He called Timothy his "dearly beloved son," as he did later *Titus* and showed concern over their health and what they ate and drank. *Philemon* he addressed as a brother—was it because they were nearer in age or because Philemon was a Greek?

Timothy had been freed from prison and was the scribe for Paul's letter to the *Hebrews*, written from Italy. *James* and *Peter* and *John*, as well as *Jude*, brother of James, wrote their own letters, some very short, blending personal news with that of the church which was their life. How brave those men were!

The *Revelation* of St. John the Divine, which ends the New Testament, was un-understandable to me as a twelve-year old and remains so today. The series of vivid out-of-this-world tableaux it presented illumined my dreams for a long time. Daddy comforted me by saying that he didn't understand it either and that we were in the company of many learned men and women who had studied and read for years trying to interpret the message they felt lay within it.

Freed of guilt by his words, I could then focus on the monetary aspects of my deal. My grandmother paid up promptly and some of her hope for me was fulfilled. I can't remember at all what happened to the twenty-five dollars, but I DO remember reading the Bible!

# *Four*

# Last Arkansas Home

## *Sew a Fine Seam*

I GREW UP in a book-ridden household with reading material shelved, stacked, and scattered everywhere. As soon as I could hold them, I was given books of my own—cloth pages, highly colored at first and then big board-backed nursery rhymes and folk tales. *Peter Rabbit* was a small, square, green-bound volume with my favorite illustration of Peter caught in the fence. I also had free access to my parents' library, and I really can't remember when I didn't know the excitement of words and reading.

All this familiarity with books rather complicated things when I started to school. I was to attend a small experimental school on the campus—a school so small that it held even-numbered grades one year, odd-numbered grades the next. I had a half year or so of kindergarten after we moved from Kansas to Arkansas and so was considered ready for first grade. But I had read everything the little first-grade library contained and was more than holding my own in arithmetic and other subjects. There was no second grade for me, and after considerable discussion between my parents and the teachers, it was decided to try me in third grade. After all, it was an experimental school and it was very small. It was all very friendly, and I had no particular interest in what grade I attended so long as there was plenty to read and do. Mary Frances, my cross-the-street neighbor, and I were about the same age and in the same grade, so it was very comfortable and familiar.

At Peabody we missed many disciplined methods of learning such as "times tables" and all kinds of measures—solid, liquid, linear—but we always knew where and how to look for the information we needed and we picked up vast amounts of trivia, useful and curious. "Problem solving" was a big thing with us.

In eighth grade, the imminence of high school began to be important, and various plans were set in motion by our teachers to make us ready for a more formal course of study the following year. I experienced my first year of French, challenging as presented in a deep southern accent by Miss Booth, whose eccentrically dyed hair shone with a metallic lustre when the sun struck it. Although I proved to be no linguist, I took part in a French play in June and was ready to start high school with a fully accredited unit in French. *C'est magnifique!*

Sad to say, my success did not carry over into Home Economics, a "broadening" course offered Peabody School students by the university department and taught by members of their regular staff. The first semester "Cooking," as it was plainly called then, went by very well, and I learned how to make a smooth white sauce, separate eggs without breaking the yolks and came upon a great fudge recipe that I cherished for years. Both boys and girls took Cooking and it was lots of fun. Eating had always been one of life's genuine pleasures for me, and I particularly relished the little feasts that followed each class session when we gobbled up our triumphs or failures.

But Sewing was a different matter. Taught by the head of the Home Ec department, a spinster of early middle age who apparently hated young girls, this class became a disaster for me. Sensing her disapproval of us, we almost at once began to harbor rebellion against her strict regime. No advocate of the experimental approach to learning, Miss Palmer had rules as unbending as her corseted back. We were not to talk with each other as we sewed; we were forbidden to borrow sewing articles from one another (if you had left your scissors at home, you had to go to her desk to "sign out" a pair or do no cutting that day); you must ask her permission to proceed from one step to another in making your designated article. We mocked her tightly rolled bun of hair, her slightly bulging blue eyes, and her severe speech.

I was in trouble with the first real assignment after we completed our samplers of stitches. My "even" and "uneven" bastings had resembled each other too closely and had been ripped out and re-done until the linen on which I worked was pulled and gray with overuse. Finally, however, Miss Palmer gave me permission to forge ahead with the next project.

This was to be a laundry bag. The size and material (cretonne) were set forth; length of cord for the casing was designated. The bag was to be made of material that had no up or down in design so that a fold would make no difference in its appearance. Needless to say, instructions were to be followed with no variance.

Mary Frances and I went shopping together to Campbell and Bell's, where she found a pretty rose strewn "allover" design. Her mother would love it, she was sure. And I had spotted just what I wanted for Mother—a blue and white cretonne, its design clearly taken from the willow-ware plates my mother liked so much. True, it had a clear up-and-down. Folded across the length of the cloth, half the Chinese people, trees, bridges, and boats were forced to stand upside down. But my experimental school training stood me in good stead (I thought). This was only a problem, I reasoned, and one easily solved. All I had to do was cut the material in half, make a seam across the bottom (I envisioned a neat French seam of which Miss Palmer would be proud) and, *voilà*, everyone and everything on both sides of my bag would be upright. I bought the handsome fabric and took it to class next day.

There I stepped out of line again: cut the material and sewed the necessary seam without asking permission. It looked good—just as I had visualized it—and so I went ahead with the side seams and then took it to my instructor for approval before stitching the casing.

A storm fell on my head: "You are a willful, disobedient child!" she said angrily. "Please tell me why you failed to follow instructions!"

Confused and embarrassed, I slunk away to my assigned table, finished my laundry bag (still thinking it looked quite nice) and turned it in with the others done as she had directed. It came back to me with no grade, but Mother treasured it as I had believed she would.

Things went from bad to worse. I was certainly not a born seamstress, but I tried—hard! I really wanted to learn to sew. And with the next article, an apron as I remember, I managed to do as I was told.

Then came the final assignment—a choice between making a nightgown or a slip. It is revealing of the times that either piece of lingerie was to be made of fine white cambric. I chose a slip. True, it had five panels— one in front, one on each side, and two in back—but the fitting of those pieces into a shapely whole was a challenge, and the seams (French, of course) were short. Mary Frances took a nightgown for her project, long seams and all. It was a long, hard process, and we worked doggedly to get those pieces to lie smoothly with each other and to take shape on us. At last we were ready for permission to stitch the final seams. Then Miss Palmer descended upon us, shears in hand. She had spied a fullness in a seam, she said. The offending garments were soon laid out on the cutting table, and our instructor went to work. The two seams in Mary Frances' nightgown were quickly trimmed off—to be completely done over. It took her longer to dispatch all five of mine, and when I saw the narrow strips that she had left me, I realized that the new seams would have to be minute, indeed.

Mary Frances and I soberly began to sew up our diminished garments. Taking the narrowest possible seams, we hadn't the heart to try the clothes on again before they were finished. And when we did take that fatal step, my friend found that she could barely sit in her nightgown but only by taking the smallest steps could she walk. My five-paneled wonder was like a sausage casing for my skinny string-bean figure. By letting out all my breath and wriggling carefully, I could pull it on. Talcum powder helped! I could not possibly sit in it.

Miss Palmer's rule was inflexible. If one made a garment that was unwearable, one failed the course. I received an "F" in Sewing.

Mother came to my rescue. I had never before known her to go to school on a mission of any kind other than attendance at our parties and programs, but without any prior discussion she paid a carefully arranged visit to Miss Palmer. And when she returned home, she brought the news that my "F" had been softened to an "E," which at that time stood for "Incomplete." I was to make a "wearable" garment during the summer under Mother's supervision. It would be graded in the fall by Miss Palmer.

And so I entered high school with my unit of French and my retrieved credit in Home Economics, wondering what lay ahead.

## We Move Again

My parents bought the Hill Street house in June, 1921, paying $6250.00 for the nine room, two-story home with two baths, a spacious screened porch off the kitchen, a deep, dark basement, and two attics. It was shaded by maples and elms and sat high on a terrace like the Dickson Street house. The quarter of a block property made room for a storehouse, a smokehouse, a large rambling barn, part of which had been made over into a garage, and left room for Will Carr's thriving vegetable garden. One tall elm was the best swing tree we had ever had. The "bag swing" Will hung for us had to be mounted from a rickety ladder and its wide arc took me high into the sky.

I did have to give up my own cherished playhouse, but I was getting older; I had been in high school for a year and I loved the idea, as my parents did, of living in an owned rather than a rented home. Our houses had been rented since the move to Arkansas, and when the Dickson Street rent was raised to an astronomical sixty dollars a month, Mother and Daddy decided that it was time to become householders again.

While Daddy was busy with summer school, Mother supervised the moving and storing of our furnishings, canned fruit and vegetables, and winter clothes to the Gill house, as our new home was still known. Actually the Gills had stipulated in the sale that they would remain in residence throughout the summer. We were given two rooms for storage. The first of August, our family took off for Evanston, where we spent a month enjoying all the urban delights Chicago could offer. Ringling Brothers circus in Grant Park by the lake was a special wonder. My father was never so happy as when he was walking the streets and breathing the air of a city, and he shared that excitement with us in the parks, the Loop, and the Art Institute.

Daddy continued his busy schedule of institute speaking and was back and forth between Evanston and Ohio, Indiana, and Texas until the middle of September, when we were all officially at home at 31 South Hill Street. The Gills had remained in the house for five days after we returned from Illinois!

My father celebrated residence in our new home by coming down with a severe case of erysipelas, complicated by painful tonsilitis and quinsy. His fever raged around one hundred five degrees and Dr. Ellis called at the house, sometimes twice a day. Daddy's health was never robust, and I marvel at the tenacity he summoned to keep going day after day. Although the radical surgery he had had earlier eased his abdominal discomfort somewhat, I have vivid memories of seeing him literally writhe and hearing him cry out in the anguish of "gall bladder colic." Quick to sense and relieve another's pain, he was slow to admit his own. A shake of his head and the wry comment, "P O M J (Poor Old Man Jewell)" assessed the situation when he was ill or life went amiss. He was a courageous stoic.

## Rich Man / Poor Man

Brought up in a small college town in the South, where the culture dictated that three topics were taboo, I never heard discussions, public or private, about age, money or sex. Birthdays were acknowledged, even named and counted in the case of children, but all adults were considered to be "of a certain age," "getting on," or, with a slow shake of the head, "failing." There was no talk of a midlife crisis then or of the fearful forties.

Mother and Daddy were liberal people even by today's standards, but sex was never mentioned so far as I can remember. I knew that there were boys and girls who grew up to be men and women. Magically they fell in love, married, and, in the course of time, generally became parents—a privileged state that permitted them to make all sorts of lordly decisions, mostly about their children. I was a girl. I dreamed about the majestic period which lay far ahead but would naturally arrive and confer upon me all its benefits and power.

As far as money was concerned, all I knew was that we had very little. A frequent response to my brother's and my requests for some special treat or trinket was, "I'm sorry, honey (or son), we can't afford it." That simple statement seemed to end the matter. The word "poor" crossed no one's lips. And truly we were not poor—it was just that everyone I played with and the majority of my parents' friends enjoyed a wealth we did not have. Bankers, lawyers, doctors, merchants seemed to me to be made of money. As a university professor and administrator, my father received a salary so small as to be hardly noticeable. During two years of state insolvency, when salary vouchers issued by the State of Arkansas could not be cashed at less than a fifty per cent discount at any bank, my father kept his accumulated pay checks in his safe deposit box and hoped for better times. Somehow he managed to support two households (my physician grandfather had become an invalid). Their three, my grandparents and the widowed daughter-in-law of a foster son years older than my father, added to our five: Mother, Daddy, Jimmie, Baby Keith, born during the critical time close after World War I, and I, plus a cook who lived in and a yard man who lived out made a heavy burden for a school teacher in what was probably

called "reduced" or "straitened" circumstances. Looking
back at this period from a more understanding view-
point, I realize that Daddy must have made ends meet
through the fees paid him for his many public speaking
engagements. A talented and popular lecturer, he was
often away overnight, on weekends, or for longer in the
summer, when he had week-long contracts at the nu-
merous teacher's conferences that preceded summer
schools on university campuses. He was a psychologist
at a time when Freud was just beginning to be heard of,
having visited America on his initial trip to Clark
University in Worcester, Massachusetts, where he was
hosted by my father's mentor, G. Stanley Hall. Daddy's
topics, such as "The Busy Quart and The Lazy Gallon,"
were informative and instuctional, always geared to the
local scene, and enlivened by his ability as a humorist
and story teller. People who heard him remembered the
stories he told for years, and they also remembered the
point he had been making with the story. Volumes of
correspondence over the years attested to that.

From my point of extreme self-interest, Daddy's trips
were all to the good because of the gifts he brought on his
return. Being in New York, Chicago, and St. Louis was
a great pleasure for him, and between engagements and
bookshops he spent more time choosing dresses and
shoes for Mother and me and suits for Jimmie than another man might have done. Flaunting a pair of brown
shoes with high tops of fine khaki-colored serge from
Marshall Field's when my friends were in their customary black laced winter shoes was a status experience
that I savored to the fullest.

In my wardrobe I usually had to recognize what we
could NOT afford. Looking back, I realize all that my
mother did to make her economies exciting rather than
limiting. She bought yardage and ribbon, lace and no-
tions on special sales at Campbell and Bell's, where the

little baskets ran on a complicated overhead trolley system from clerk to office and back again. Stored in a particular closet, their bounty was turned out twice a year, autumn and spring, when Mrs. Seamster, the dressmaker, came to live for a week in our guestroom. She and Mother designed, cut, and sewed every day, spreading out the remnants and casting a sharp eye at color and textures, deciding what would go with what and whether there was "enough" for a particular pattern. Sometimes they used thin tissue paper patterns that fell softly from their envelopes and then seemed to expand until, folded more intricately than road maps, they had to be virtually stuffed back into their flat holders. But most often there were one, two, or three pictures clipped from magazines, catalogs, or newspapers that Mother would eye intermittently as she held up piece after piece of material to see how it "hung" and how it looked "with" another scrap.

She achieved some notable designs: a rosebud broadcloth striped with heavier threads and made into a severely tailored schooldress to tone down its romantic print; a waffle-like plisse in a deep coral. Mother had a great eye for color. My all-time favorite, however, was a black dotted swiss (permitted me when all my highschool friends were in white or pastel summer dresses). A snug bodice with a square neckline, its short sleeves finished with deep ruffles of black taffeta ribbon, topped a full gathered skirt that had the same ribbon used as insertion halfway to the knees. This triumph resulted from several short remnants of dotted swiss and a bolt of four inch ribbon. In it I felt like a queen!

Economies showed themselves at the table where we became charter members of the Clean Plate Club before the organization existed. Most vegetables came from our garden, planted and tended by Will Carr. That they were seasonal meant that we feasted on whatever was ripe and ready for the table. A favorite summer supper was made up of platters of roasting ears (usually the sweet, irregular Country Gentleman) dripping with butter, another platter of rich red tomato slices, crisp bacon, and cornbread. In winter we had meatloaf about once a week, baked potatoes, beets, and cinnamon drenched baked apples for dessert. No wonder we cleaned our plates! There was little need for talk at our table about the "starving Armenians," although I heard them mentioned frequently when my friends were being urged to polish off their plates. We were required to eat what was served us and leave no "courtesy bites" on our plates. The only time, in fact, that I ever remember saying flat out that I would NOT do something was when I told my father that I positively would not eat the very small portion of spinach he was spooning onto my plate. His eyebrows lifted; he looked me steadily in the eye. "Oh, yes, I think you will," he said quietly. My rebellion at an end, I did!

Daddy, too, was ingenious at making ends meet in an interesting rather than humble manner. Bates Bros. Grocery was scarcely a fancy food market, neither was Gollaher's, up the street. My father's appetite for a wider variety on his table led to his initiation of a sort of cooperative buying group, made up largely of faculty families as poor income-wise as we were. Oysters were ordered from Boston and Baltimore, salmon and halibut from Seattle. Before the days of refrigerator cars, much less flash freezing, these seafood delicacies came in five gallon tins packed in real ice, which melted down to salt brine and a few frosty chips by the end of their journey. My favorite Tokay grapes came from California just in time for my October birthday. They were packed in sawdust and required careful washing. Idaho furnished potatoes and celery. Ohio supplied honey, both in the comb and strained, as well as queen bees for my father's hives. Each shipment meant many telephone calls and

the arrival at our home of subscribers (friends and ac-
quaintances) carrying their own jars or tins or sacks or
roasters depending on the nature of the food that had
come. There was lots of laughter and frivolous talk as
cutting, weighing, and measuring took place. In exchange for the idea and the enterprise, my parents had
their portions free.

Somehow my parents kept us afloat, supported my
grandparents and Aunt Lucy, kept two full-time
helpers, Elizabeth or Mrs. Donnelly in the house and
Will Carr, who had "toting privileges." No one was ever
turned away hungry. I suppose Mother fed at least ten
people a day; how she did it, I can't imagine.

She also entertained generously and with great flair,
whether for Daddy's students and faculty or their personal friends, town and gown. Mother had relatively little interest in everyday cooking but was a superb holiday
cook, and she loved "theme" parties for which she could
design and prepare favors, place cards, and special
menus. I guess now that the frequency of everyday
chipped beef in gravy, macaroni and cheese, or that
great treat, pork and beans, helped even off the budget.
At the time, of course, I didn't even wonder.

My personal allowance before I was in high school
was twenty-five cents a month. I still have one of the account books that I had to present on the first of each
month in order to receive that princely sum. Each page
is decorated with what I evidently felt was a timely mo-
tif: April carries a parade of tiny umbrellas under neat
dots of rain; May has a bouquet of improbable flowers;
July's firecrackers face each other with fuses sparkling.
The entries include a weekly contribution of five cents for
Sunday School, so I had little left to squander. However,
some earnings are recorded: weeding and raking
brought in a little extra income. It was a tight economy
and a rich life.

## What War First Meant To Me

As a member of a distinctly non-martial family, I am frequently surprised to find what powerful exclamation marks war has made in the ongoing history of our clan. Brought up in the South at a time when the grandparents of almost every child I knew were reliving and retelling their memories and personal tales of the Civil War, I recognized it as the classic prototype of conflict. That The War Between The States had been lost by the Confederacy only enlarged the tales of heroism and martyrdom. That the fighting had been over issues and values that sometimes divided families and set brother against brother made the reminiscing bitter. The widely held central issue: that WE were invaded, that WE had to fight to protect our homes and our women made the long ago battles seem as close as the day's sunshine.

At school in American History classes, we launched into The War shortly after school began in September. Brief mention was made of Virginia, Plymouth, Salem, Boston, the Thirteen Colonies and the War of the Revolution. I always hoped to linger there a while in order to talk about the heavy rusted sword in its cracked leather scabbard that I knew some family member had wielded in pursuit of colonial freedom. My ancestors on both sides had been settlers in this country for well over a hundred years at the time of the Revolution, living in the countryside near Boston—the Keiths in West Bridgewater, Massachusetts, where the first manse in the United-States-to-be had been built for the Reverend James Keith. The young Congregational minister had brought his little flock with him from Aberdeen, Scotland when he came at the age of eighteen to settle in a new land. The Jewells, part of the extended family of Bishop James Jewell in England, had established themselves in Quincy. A deed of land transfer to them is recorded there prior to 1650.

When I first visited New England, stood on the little bridge in Concord, looked across the velvet-green parade ground in Lexington, heard warm summer rain pound the roof of the saltbox manse in Bridgewater, I felt such waves of atavistic fervor that I could have swung the sword myself. The Reverend Keith evidently had no such warlike impulses and during or after the French and Indian wars had sheltered King Philip's wife and child in his manse before their escape southward.

But all of this had taken place centuries ago, and I had not yet been in Massachusetts. The Civil War and all its battles, its generals, its skirmishes, its tattered, starving army was all about me. Our history class emerged from the campaigns late in May or early June, when our teacher of the year hurriedly mentioned that there had been generations of Americans since then, that a World War had been won (largely, she implied, through American bravery) to save the world for democracy, and that this vision of everlasting peace was ours to keep and enjoy forever.

Outside the classroom we searched for stubby, blunt bullets and small "minnie balls" in the peach orchards of Cane Hill (where the Battle had been fought) and on lazy afternoons walked by Miss Amanda's house to pass the time. We never tired of inspecting carefully the rosy pink brick of its wall toward the garden where a large circular patch of more recently laid red slabs lay like a blood stain. That stain mended The Hole left by the cannon ball that had shot through the house in front of Miss Amanda's sister/cousin/aunt as she came down the curving stair, her baby in her arms! The story varied in its small details, but its body remained the same. We knew Miss Amanda and feared her, a spare, grey-haired spinster with a tart tongue who tolerated no nonsense. Each time we saw the stain and heard or retold the story, shivers ran up our spines. What would it feel like to have a hole blasted through your own house wall? The houses, the gardens, the fields, the land itself had been threatened.

My own family history of the Civil War presented some problems. The kindergarten classmate who called me a Damn Yankee on the first day of school because I was from Kansas didn't know even half of my Northern heritage. Mother's face, on that occasion, was white and her arms had a particular tension around me. She was fiercely proud of her father, who as a very young recruit had fought for the Union Army. He had been wounded and the letters home he had written during months in a field hospital were carefully wrapped in a white silk scarf in the small round wooden chest covered with deerskin that was polished with time and travel.

On my father's side there were the stories of my great grandfather, Daniel Coe, who had volunteered his home in the Catskills as an underground railway station for black people escaping slavery as they stole furtively to Canada. After The War, Grandpa Coe had set up a lumber mill in Talledega, Alabama, where he hoped to provide employment for freshly-freed blacks and impoverished white men alike. This Utopian dream ended after several years of community misunderstanding and persecution when the Klan set fire to the mill and burned it to the ground.

It was not always easy to grow up Yankee in Dixie, and I learned early to keep a great many beliefs and opinions to myself. I finally understood why Mother could belong to the DAR but not to the Daughters of the Confederacy, and I greatly regretted not being asked to pass mints and napkins at the whipped cream and petit fours laden teas of the latter group as I had always done for the former. Then, too, Mother called our laundress

Mrs. Wellington and would employ no black help inside the house. She preferred teaching young white girls from the mountains to cook and serve and answer the door. For years we treasured Elizabeth's comment as Mother showed her which fork to set where, "Miz Jewell, you sure is a heap of trouble to yourself!"

My father was the one who bridged the gap and helped us cross it. Born in Tennessee, brought up in Kansas, the most tolerant man I have ever known and a passionate believer in mankind, he loved and was loved by students and townspeople alike. His tolerance was neither lazy nor ignorant. He was simply and profoundly at ease with Will Carr, our black yard man, and Dr. Ellis, our respected family doctor and Klan member. Both were Daddy's trusted friends and cherished the time spent with him.

To my ears, steeped in the all-around-me lore of the war fought between North and South in the rose gardens and peach orchards of people I knew, foreign battle cries sounded truly far away. My first knowledge of World War I must have come through hearing my parents talk about Cousin Oliver's becoming a soldier. I knew about soldiers; when I was going home from school, watching the ROTC parade over the broad, green grass that spread from under the maple trees on campus was one of my great pleasures. They moved so briskly, turned and wheeled and stopped with a smart click of their heels. "Present arms!" had a special flourish. To a six year-old, they appeared very stylish. I loved the flags and the bugles. Lucky Oliver! How sad for him I was when they told me he had become ill and could not be a soldier any more. (Oliver had contracted TB in training camp and was to spend more than the war years in a military hospital. When he regained his health he settled in Arizona, then in Texas and amassed a fortune.)

The newspapers sported heavy black headlines featuring the Huns and their atrocities. My reading vocabulary expanded with "submarines" and "Lusitania." How wonderful that the world was to be saved for Democracy! (Whatever Democracy might be.) Service flags hung in many windows and I grieved that we could not show one. Sometimes the blue stars were changed to gold ones. Mrs. Trimble's son would never come home again to gorge on her good biscuits. My mother wore a grey Red Cross uniform with a flowing white veil and rolled bandages. She looked beautiful.

Most exciting was the music. "Over There" could be heard day and night. I practiced the stammer required for "K-K-K-Katie" until my parents forbade it—fearing, rightly, that I hoped to make the halting speech my own. (I failed to understand my parents' disapproval of my earnest attempts to become an accomplished stutterer.) "Mademoiselle from Armentiers" was too risque for public singing and had to be practiced in private, far from adult ears. Oh, it was a glorious time, a fantasy, carrying none of the weight and reality of the Civil War, where people had been actually shot at!

## River Scene

Climbing out of the swimming hole from the slow-moving water, brown as the water moccasin that had once slithered under my foot on the muddy bank, I promised myself that I'd lie on the grass in the sun and bake happily for a while before we went home. I preferred earth to water anyway since a childhood experience in Colorado that had brought me close to drowning and frightened me badly. The quiet, partially dammed pool considered safe for swimming was a far cry from the clean, rushing current of most of the mountain rivers. I didn't like it. I turned and stretched in the heat, felt the itch of grass against my back, closed my eyes against the sun glare. Limp as a cat, I gave myself to the earth.

But my best friend kept calling to me from the water. Brought up on Lake Michigan, Ruth was an excellent swimmer, had coached with Johnny Weismuller of Tarzan fame, and was a real water baby. Neither she nor her younger brother, Bud, the prankish, teasing bane of our existence, could understand my apprehension about the water. The whole teenage gang had brought picnic lunches and bathing suits for a day on the river. They joined Ruth's plea, "Just one more dip before we go home!"

I gave in, waded through the shallows and plunged into the deep water, using my trusty side-stroke to join the others. I was almost there when suddenly someone swam up behind me and strong hands on my shoulders pushed me under. It was Bud, two years younger but as tall as I and full of his emerging strength. He mounted my shoulders, locked his knees under my chin and pushed my head forward. Frantic, I tried to tear his legs apart, free myself from his heavy body. He was a great practical joker and evidently enjoyed my struggles. Fearless of the water as a dolphin and almost equally agile, he kept his tight hold on my neck, plunging and rolling under water with me fighting below him. I struggled, tried to tread water, but his weight was too much for me. When I tried to bite his encircling legs, brown water filled my mouth. Soon I ran out of breath. My ears rang. My throat was strangely dry. My chest was swollen with its need for air. I could feel the brown water inside me as well as out. An overpowering fatigue began to close in. My legs would no longer pump; my arms were limp as I clawed feebly at Bud's legs. The world of water grew grey, then black.

Fortunately, Bud's fun diminished as my struggles grew weaker, and when my body dropped flaccid under him and became a dead weight, he realized that the game was over. He started to swim away but when I failed to surface, he knew something was wrong. Calling for help, he dove to find me on rotting logs at the bottom of the pool. They pulled me out, rolled me on the bank and went to work—"Out goes the bad air—"

I regained consciousness finally, nauseous and sore, nasal passages and throat raw, aching and terrified. They carried me to a car, drove me to a hospital and expert care. Really, I should have stayed on the bank!

## Strawberry Shortcake, Huckleberry Pie

If Mother had not been so commanding in her order that I abandon my activity on the gridiron for all time, I would possibly have emerged as the first young feminist to integrate the game of football on a sexual basis. University High School had at most 120 students and relatively few were "out for football"; fielding a full team was not easy. I would have loved to offer myself up to their need for a running back, but it was evident that this was not going to happen. Even my erstwhile teammates had changed attitudes toward my playing. They were now intent on the "schedule," full of talk about uniforms and equipment, exceedingly male in point of view.

(The term "macho" was not yet in use in Anglo-Saxon Arkansas.)

And so I was relegated to the sidelines. The team played its home games on the University practice field and practiced wherever there was an unused fringe of turf. Five or six of us, the others appearing to be far more interested in individual players than in the game, raced up and down what could be loosely called the "sidelines" on practice days. There were no bleachers to cramp our semi-participation or keep us in a spectator/player framework.

On game days we alternated between sprinting up and down the field beside the players and shaking homemade pompons (which we called "pompoMs") to the exaggerated rhythm of:

> *Strawberry shortcake,*
> *Huckleberry pie—*
> *V-I-C-T-O-R-Y*
> *Are we in it?*
> *Well, I guess!*
> *We're the kids from*
> *the U-H-S!*

I imagine we had the unspoken belief that if things got tough for our side, we could simply close in on the opposition and smother them with numbers.

University High somehow managed a full schedule of games, and although we were always, as I remember, on the losing end of the local competition with the larger, stronger, more affluent Fayetteville High School, we sometimes went so far out of town as to cross state lines in our search for opponents. Our principal and other administrators were somewhat distressed by our reputation as an academic high school, "full of professors' kids" and went to some lengths to see that extra-curricular activities received full support.

On one memorable occasion, we even rented a truck with a long flat bed hemmed in by tall stakes and woven with rope or cable to take us to Oklahoma, where we were needed, we felt, to support our team. Stilwell, a small town of less than 2,000 inhabitants, lay not far from the state boundary—about sixty miles from Fayetteville. Their team had been talked up as rough and tough. It even had some Indians on it! Clearly, an all-out effort was called for here.

About twenty of us gathered early on the morning of the game, laden with lunches and blankets—there were no seats in the truck. Two teachers, one the driver, sat in the truck's cab. The second, a young practice teacher, was the "girls' chaperone." She had to be young to imagine that a trip like ours would be fun—either that or she had been conscripted.

Sixty miles over bumpy, mostly gravel roads took their toll. We talked, cheered, and sang, but we could barely summon up our pride and voices to chant our fight song, composed to the popular strains of "Margie," as we drove along the dusty main street of Stilwell to the fairgrounds, where the game was to be played.

There were Indians on the team and sitting in the rough board bleachers. There was also what seemed to us the entire population of Stilwell. And there was no nonsense about hospitality or good sportsmanship or cheer. Every Sooner present was on hand to see that his team won—reduced those smart nincompoops from across the state line to pulp. Although they stayed physically in the stands, they figuratively ran the sidelines beside their players, and with deadly intent. We were awed and frightened and huddled close together in our small share of the benches. Our players looked tight-lipped and white and very fragile beside the sturdy farm boys, whose broad shoulders and barrel chests thrust out their bodypads.

The game began with the familiar whistle and the two teams pushed back and forth, feeling each other out. No score for the first quarter. The pushing and shoving got rougher; the tackles were brutal—noses bled in bright streams, cleat-cut shins added their ribbons of color. No score in the second quarter.

The teams left the field in frustration and huddled on opposite sides of the field. They drank from big sponges and then held the sponges against the backs of their necks. The coaches went around to individual players, slapped backs, embraced their shoulders, gave encouragement, criticism, advice. Then they called the team together while we strained to hear. Only a few words, "Keep going—You can do it—Fight! Fight! Fight!" came through.

The second half was more savage than the first. Stilwell was used to winning; our team, not always on the losing side, had its pride. They were outweighed, outmatched physically in every way, but they had not used the varsity field and watched the varsity teams practice for nothing. They had strategy and "play plans" on their side. No score in the third quarter.

The teams changed position on the field. The air was electric. Officials no longer called small infringements; they were too busy separating slugging matches, preventing public mayhem. Back and forth in the clouds of dust on the unturfed playing field, the players ground out their downs. Minutes only remained on the clock. Ground plays ended almost before they began. Each snap of the ball seemed to come after an offside (uncalled) by someone.

And then our quarterback called a short pass and our whole team seemed to pile up as interference. We thought the receiver was down—but no, out of the melee, heading for the side of the field tore Bill, the fastest man on the team. Other players picked themselves up, started after him; some vicious blocks were thrown; one fleet Indian was on his heels. Ten yards, twenty, and Bill crossed the goal line inches ahead of his pursuer and fell to a crouch protecting the ball. No grandstanding wave of the ball in that game.

No conversion was possible. The officials simply could not get the teams lined up in any kind of a formation. The gun went off while private fights waged over the field.

The crowd, with a low, animal-like roar surged onto the field. Our players were locked in a tight wedge trying to get to the cars that had driven them over. We ran as best we could for our truck. Men, women, children blocked our way or tried to lay hands on us. Perhaps the best way to sum it up is to say that we were truly "run out of town." In Stilwell, one played for keeps.

We had our pride, too, and the victory—unbelievably—was ours. As soon as it was apparent that we had distanced ourselves safely from our enraged hosts, we stood up in the truck and to the unlikely melody of "Margie" left Stilwell singing,

> *Vars'ty, we're always rooting for you,*
> *Vars'ty—*
> *When at eve the setting sun*
> *Sees the work the team has done—*
> *Oh, Vars'ty, Vars'ty, you've won!*

## Mrs. Donnelly

*She was a short round*
*dumpling of a woman,*
*upholstered in sprigged*
*gray cotton, long to the*
*floor from an earlier style.*
*Did she have legs? We*
*daren't peek.*

*Her apron, cinched tight*
*in the middle, separated*
*bosom from hips and made*
*a clean white statement*
*down the front. What*
*would spill over if*
*the drawstring were cut?*

*Gray hair matched the sprigs*
*of her calico dress, its wiry*
*strands frizzling to escape*
*the hairpin skewers in*
*her tight bun. Eyes, never*
*at rest, saw everything,*
*forgave nothing.*

*She was Black Irish, keening*
*and wailing, mourning flesh*
*and the world and all who lived in*
*it. Each black day began with*
*a curse called on someone:*
*her family, our family,*
*the Pope or the milkman.*

*From back of the door to the*
*pantry, we shivered and heard*

*her, heard our names called and*
*knew how close we were—and she*
*was our cook and we'd plagued her*
*and teased her just to see the*
*red anger choke up her face.*

*She was not to be pleased,*
*though we seldom tried, but*
*we'd watched our parents*
*attempt it and fail—praise*
*from my father bounced*
*back as if struck—"Ought to*
*be good, had good things in it."*

*Even when Mother stood close*
*by the stove, Mrs. D's tartness*
*popped quick from her mouth,*
*"If I was in your way,*
*I'd get out," she said and*
*clattered the kettle to make*
*her point clear.*

*Will Carr*

It was summer vacation—a lazy, dreaming day in the Ozark sunshine. Bees floated drowsily around the honey-suckle screen that half-hid the slanting doors to the cellar. The nectar-heavy trumpets hung so close together that their fragrance carried all through the house, and once in a while the ruby throats of hummingbirds would flash in the sun as they dipped their long beaks into the narrow bells. The house was quiet—

Daddy was over on the campus busy with summer school; my brother had gone off to play with Little Bill Dunn, a friend and neighbor; Mrs. Donnelly had vanished into her room until dinner preparations would call her out, and Mother was napping. I felt a very special aloneness as I lay on the sofa in the library reading *Girl of the Limberlost*. What a dramatic life she led! Why didn't anything ever happen to me?

The whirr of Will Carr's lawnmower came through the window close to the swing tree, the big elm nearest to the house. That meant that he was almost finished with the lawn and would take his sickle and go out into the vegetable garden that was his pride. I loved to see him slash away at the tall grass that grew against the fence. It fell in green swathes from the shining crescent blade. Will hated a dull tool and kept that blade well honed. Will kept everything just right and he knew how to do anything you asked. He was the one who had hung that swing so high and on such a long rope that I had a tremendous arc of flight when I pumped hard. He was the one, too, who had carried me to the house for help when the swing board caught me in the face.

Will was our yard man—tall, broad, long-legged, head held high. Daddy often said, "Will is one of the finest men I've ever known." And he would take a cup of coffee out to Will and the two men, black and white, would talk in the shade of a big maple, long after the cups were empty. Will never came inside except to do windows or move furniture or trunks. Mother ordinarily allowed no black help in the house and said she felt uncomfortable with the way they expected to be treated. Our laundress, Lily to everyone else, was Mrs. Wellington to Mother. Mother was Yankee, a proud Jayhawker from Kansas. Cantankerous old John Brown would have met a kindred spirit in her rugged independence. She didn't flaunt her Northern background—Mother didn't flaunt—but she did live up to her own standards, complex as it made our living at times.

We usually had white hired girls from the mountains for cooking and inside help, but Elizabeth had left us to marry her Ozark sweetheart, Jerd, and Mrs. Donnelly had come to cook for us. Mrs. Donnelly was short and round and looked like a calico-clad dumpling, but she was keening Irish and held the firm belief that the world was really our purgatory and all of us were doomed. She was hard to live with and her particular grievance, voiced loudly and often, was that she had to serve lunch to Will on the back screened porch where he ate alone. Slamming his plate down on the table and jerking it off almost before he had finished, she stomped around half the afternoon in a fine fit of temper. It had been a relief when she mounted the steps to her room after doing the lunch dishes.

Daddy said, "Honey, she just doesn't understand" when I asked him about it and told him how polite Will was when he thanked her, always, and told her what good food she cooked. Daddy reminded me that even when he tried to compliment Mrs. Donnelly after dinner or a party, she would grumble, "Ought to be good, had good things in it."

"Some people find it very hard just to live," Daddy commented. I knew who he meant!

There was always so much to wonder about. Eager as I was to find out more about Elnora Comstock and the moths she collected in the Limberlost, I had almost fallen asleep to the rumble of the lawnmower, the afternoon heat, and my puzzling thoughts about Mrs. Donnelly and Will. I nodded and shook myself awake. Mother's footsteps came down the stairs. Her nap was over, too. Maybe we could have some lemonade.

Before I could get to the kitchen, I heard a knock on the back porch door. Mother was there before me and

Will Carr stood outside. He was holding his left forearm tight with the other hand. Blood surged between the fingers. " 'Scuse me, Miz Jewell, but I need help." It wasn't the sight of the blood that shocked me. I had shed my own bright drops that time with the swing and once when a jump barefoot had landed on well-hidden broken glass. Grownups had talked to Mother in disapproving tones about tomboys and lockjaw that time.

But this was different. Maybe I wasn't ready to know what I learned that day. Maybe I was. Will's face looked gray and his eyes were sort of shallow like our collie's when he got hit by the car. My mother caught her breath. Will's sickle, glancing off some rock or stake, had slashed through skin and muscle to the hard white bone. Tendons shone almost blue against the tide of blood as it poured over the sweat-polished black skin. Silent and numb with shock, I stood watching. My stomach heaved. His blood looked just like mine but richer, more vital. Why had no one ever told me? All blood is red.

And there was even more to learn. My mother reached for a clean towel, handed it to Will or rather draped it over the dripping fingers. "Get my car keys, quickly, Margaret," she ordered. "We must get Will to Dr. Ellis as fast as we can." I turned away to go, then heard Will's voice, soft but firm, " 'Scuse me, Miz Jewell, but I don't need no doctor. Just open up that smokehouse, please, ma'am. You got the key?"

No one contradicted my mother! I whirled around to see the two of them gravely facing each other. And then Mother reached inside the kitchen door and lifted a large key off the hook where it always hung. "Come, Will," she said, as she stepped down beside the towering man, who bent over his bleeding arm. They walked to the smokehouse. Mother opened the creaking door. It was dark inside, black with soot from all the curing fires it had held and festooned with cobwebs. Will went in to a dark corner and Mother put her arm around me at the door. She felt me shiver and tightened her clasp.

It took only a minute or two before Will came back to us, his big left hand now full of soot covered cobwebs. Working quickly, he made a poultice of this fearsome stuff, patting it over the wound, pulling the flesh together, building up a heavy pad to staunch the flow of blood. Finally he let Mother wrap his arm tightly—blood, soot, cobwebs and all—in another clean towel she had asked me to get, along with an old pillowslip to tear into strips. She wrapped and tied and had Will sit down on a bench by the cistern. The honeysuckle smelled like a funeral now. Mother asked me to bring Will a cool drink of water.

I couldn't believe what I saw. My mother, whose devotion to cleanliness ordered our lives, was bandaging up handfuls of smokehouse dirt! At the bidding of Will Carr, our yard man, she was going against every principle of hygiene and medical practice that our grandfather and Dr. Ellis upheld! What about germs? What about infection? Blood poisoning? Once again she offered, "Will, I'll drive you home," and he replied with dignity, " 'Scuse me again, Miz Jewell, but I'll just set here a bit and then I'll walk home." And he did just that.

Will Carr's arm healed quickly and well for such a large wound. The scar was a deep one, purple against the ebony skin. Mother and Daddy talked about it often and discussed it with my grandfather, who used terms like folk medicine, soot, charcoal and carbon, and soft, absorbent dressings. There are many kinds of wisdom, they decided.

## Feeding the Hungry

After World War I, the one "to save the world for democracy," world events somehow punctured the cocoon of well-being that had been spun around me. By the early 20's the country was suffering post-war pain, problems of unemployment magnified by the unrest of returning veterans. Homeless men—tramps, vagrants, hoboes, they were called then—walked weary miles beside the highways, dropped off or climbed on every freight train that chugged along the track. Carrying their few possessions in battered old suitcases or rolled up in tattered blankets or bits of canvas, they began to appear at kitchen doors asking for food. The most frequent request was for a chance to work in exchange for dinner or supper. (Lunch was a little-used word and only occasionally did the men show up before noon.)

My mother, feeling herself particularly blessed by fate and circumstance, decided that her role in the recovery of the nation was destined. "No one will ever leave my home hungry!" she said, and up to that time no one ever had. She was a popular and generous hostess.

Word went out to Mrs. Donnelly in the kitchen and Will Carr in the yard that any petition for food was to be met with prompt assignment to an outside job, followed by a healthy serving of the current meal at the picnic table on the cistern top. "No work, no food," Mother decreed. "I don't want to insult their personal dignity."

Time went by. Our supplicants increased. Where once there had been one or two a week, there were now one or two a day and sometimes more. Our Irish cook rebelled—she had come to cook for us, she said, not for an army, and as for serving them—that was more than she would do for any no-good raggedy man of the road. Mrs. D was a notable complainer but Mother, with a year-old baby, two older children, and a busy faculty husband who delighted in bringing his students home with him could not do without her. I was impressed into serving the hungry men.

Never before had I seen people eat because they needed food. We sat at meals because it was mealtime and my mother "set a good table." Admonished to finish my served portions, I occasionally heard about the starving Armenians, but since it was obviously impossible for those needy people far around the globe to benefit from a tablespoonful or so of neglected mashed potatoes, the theme was never belabored by my parents. It was simply a household rule not to waste food. But these men ate like wolves. They lifted the meat to their mouths with their hands, they gulped their milk or water or iced tea, they shoveled in huge mouthfuls of potatoes, beans, tomatoes, corn. A serving of cake or pie was met with incredulous stares before it disappeared in a ravenous bite or two.

As the vagrants increased in number, Mother and Daddy wondered if there was truth in the legend of a chalked hieroglyph on the gate to inform subsequent travelers that here was a welcoming place. My brother and I checked the stone retaining wall for telltale markings. We found nothing. However, our faithful Will Carr reported to my father that we had run out of jobs. There was no more wood to cut and stack in long piles for the fireplaces; the smokehouse, barn/garage and woodshed had been whitewashed; the garden was weeded, the hedges pruned, the fences mended. The lawns had been raked almost bare. Broken bricks had been replaced in the curving walk. Windows shone from repeated washing. "Mr. Jewell," Will said, "there's nothing left for me."

And for my parents, money was running out. On a professor's salary, interrupted now and then when the state coffers ran low, my father supported two families:

his own and my invalid grandfather's. Mother's project
had been a costly one for both of them, and, rather than
relieving hunger, it had seemed to multiply those who
asked for help. My parents finally took what Daddy said
was the coward's way out—we went away for a month,
he on a speaking trip, my mother and we children to
relatives in Kansas. Will Carr was left in charge of yard
and garden, Mrs. Donnelly of house and kitchen. When
we returned, business was down to one a week or less.
My parents asked no questions.

## Growing Up

The term, "crazy mixed-up kid" was not in vogue the
year, 1920, I entered University High School, but it could
have been stretched to include me. Not that I was identi-
fiably crazy, but I was mixed-up. Eleven years old, soon
to be twelve, I was still quite a little girl, playing with
dolls in my wall-high dollhouse occasionally when I was
alone. This pastime I had begun to conceal from my
friends. I had only recently been retired, under duress,
from football, and running as a pattern of locomotion
still seemed more comfortable to me than walking.

Boys occupied a strange place in my thinking. The
ease and trust I had given them as teammates and co-
conspirators in my tomboy past had given way to a sense
of discomfort, almost suspicion. How my girl friends
could view any of these loud-voiced, gangling, foot-shuf-
fling creatures as "cute" was simply beyond my compre-
hension. How they could wonder if they had been noticed
by Jack or Boling or Edgar stretched my credulity to the

limit. Everyone I knew seemed vaguely changed. The girls whispered more and giggled constantly (if they weren't in the Girl's Room, crying their eyes out). The boys told terrible jokes and guffawed loudly or suddenly turned a dusky red and pounded each other on the back. Why was high school so different? Most of these strangers had been classmates since I started to school.

Classes were better than free time because I genuinely liked to learn, and I knew what to do in the classroom. In entrance testing I had achieved second place in the class, following closely after Frank, acknowledged to be a "brain." Algebra was quite a surprise—I had never before enjoyed any part of mathematics, but this matter of "x," an unknown, excited my curiosity. And, although I have always been a skeptic about astrology, perhaps the intriguing balance of the equations appealed to my horoscope, since I was born under the seventh sign into the house of Libra. Stanger things have happened!

It was somewhat of a relief to delve into Ancient History, a rapid survey of civilization from the Egyptian pharaohs to the Dark Ages, and let the well known and constantly studied War Between the States take care of itself for awhile.

I was taking my second year of French, and Miss Booth instituted some innovative methods such as Twenty Questions in French and student written profiles of each other, the subject to be identified after the description was read aloud to the class. *Histoire de France*, with its more advanced vocabulary was heavily interwritten and our vocabularies grew. Our accents remained deplorable.

The high point of English, always my favorite subject, was the dramatization of *Ivanhoe*. My costume cupboard still has a long, yellow-orange medieval robe of cambric, and a snapshot taken at the time shows a very melancholy Rebecca clad in that robe and veiled in dark blue, standing beside an unpeeled bentwood settee heaped with pillows. My left hand is placed dramatically between my breasts. The theater was serious business!

General Science completed my program that first year and was the bane of my existence. We had a burly instructor who bellowed out instructions and seemed so impossibly enthusiastic about *Science* that I was sure he didn't need me. And, besides, I had found fiction to be unwelcome in the field of lab notes. They were exceedingly dull as they stood, I thought. I realized that *Science* and I were not to be soulmates.

Of course, time went on and there were other classes—so many, in fact, that I rushed on to college in three years. Geometry I hated, wondering why they didn't just measure the flagpole instead of going that obscure triangulating way to discover its height. And in geometry class I sat across the aisle from Clinton Thompson, whose mother risked our outrage and mockery by calling him "Clinton," accent firmly placed on the final syllable. Clinton disliked me as much as I disliked him, and he showed it in many ways—pulling my hair which still hung in long curls, "accidentally" flipping ink on my carefully prepared papers and tripping me whenever possible. My easily exhausted patience ran out one day when I was called to the board for a demonstration and he stuck his black-ribbed ankle out between my feet. I plunged toward the floor, recovered myself, and jabbed the compass point I had conveniently at hand into his black-ribbed calf. The resulting shriek of pain was music to my ears. We were both sent to the principal's office, and, after Clinton had first aid, we were given a severe lecture about our feuding. Another term, "acting out," not in use then, might have been applicable.

My parents took this episode very seriously, and the discussion between the three of us brought floods of tears from me—even though I relished the anguish of

Clinton's wounded cry for years. It seemed to me that he really had it coming.

We were graded on deportment in those days, and I never sunk so low again. Possibly, I didn't need to because the teasing I had endured almost vanished from that day on. I had established my potential.

More classes—art, something called natural science, and, my last year in high school, an incredibly boring class in civics. That class was enough to make anyone vow never to vote for anyone or anything. Besides, I thought, Arkansas was safely in the hands of the Democratic party. (Was there another party? Incredibly, yes. At some time in the past, a Republican administration had appointed Judge Grabiel to the federal bench. He was a handsome and highly respected older man, a friend of Daddy's and an absolute wonder to me. I had been led by my classmates to believe that Republicans had horns. Daddy had a lot of explaining to do about Judge Grabiel.)

Daddy also took on the obligation of discussing with me the fact that Arkansas still had a poll tax and why it was so hard to get rid of, as well as the state's deep reluctance to use the Australian ballot. He did this after learning from me that such matters were ignored or given the once-over-lightly treatment in civics class. My father had the endearing ability, I thought, to make anything interesting.

It was my father's encouragement that led to my "going out" for debate, an unlikely activity, it appears to me now. The squad numbered only seven or eight members, and during my senior year we heatedly debated the issue of severance tax. During World War I, Arkansas bauxite had been requisitioned for aluminum, furnishing more than 90% of the ore mined in the United States. Other minerals, such as diamonds, lead-bearing galena, manganese, and cinnabar, were being exploited by outside interests. The State of Arkansas hoped to profit by taxing these raw materials. I became a passionate advocate of severance tax and found it hard to take my necessary turn pleading the negative side of the issue. Good Friday night in 1923 found me about midnight sitting disconsolately in a dimly lit railroad station. Marion Knapp, my partner, our debate coach, and I were waiting for the lonely whistle of the night train that had to be flagged down to take us home. Speaking against the severance tax that evening against Russelville High School, we had come out losers. It was to be my last debate. We were already in rehearsal for our class play, "The Spell of the Image," a who-done-it with psychic overtones.

By this time in my last year in high school, my attitude toward boys had softened. Although they were far from as exciting to me as they seemed to be to Maxine and Mary Frances and Ruth, I began to realize that boys were necessary evils. I wanted to be liked and to be like everyone else. I kept trying to find out what the formula was for popularity, and although I sadly complained to my family after an evening party at the "Y Hut," a campus recreation hall, that I was not "a social fit," I did begin to have my small innocent triumphs.

Playing something akin to Post Office at Junior Endeavor one spring night, I had my first awkward kiss. It must have been from Jimmy O'Brien, a dashing sixteen year-old from Fort Smith. How could he have chosen me? He and his sister, Fontaine, were visiting their aunt and uncle, K. C. Key and his wife. Mr. Key was a short, rotund man, secretary of the Methodist Sunday School and cashier of the First National Bank. Little did we know then that in the late 30's this estimable citizen would abscond with a major portion of the bank's funds and in the company of a "loose" woman from out of town flee to South America. He was not located for many years and extradition was never possible.

But in the early 20's, Jimmy was an exciting out-of-town beau. We must have needed each other as romantic interest without the responsibility of being together day after day. He could voice jealousy over my meeting strange boys when I went with Betty to a Girl Reserve conference in Morrilton and was entertained at a dance there. I could feel deliciously unfaithful when I went out driving the day after the dance (cutting a session of the conference) with a couple of those same strangers and for the first time in my life rode at sixty miles per hour. "Imagine, a mile a minute!" I thought and abandoned myself completely to the unbridled joy of palpable danger and wind in my hair. I did take the precaution of singing the Girl Reserve anthem, "Follow, follow, follow the gleam," under my breath as a talisman of safety.

In June after this daring adventure, I graduated from high school, so full of excitement over college in the fall and the summer trip we planned to Tennessee that my head fairly spun. Once in awhile I grew frightened—would I be rushed? What house would I choose? The structure and power of sorority life on a small campus had been well observed. In my constant struggle to be like my peers and bridge the age gap between us, I saw membership in a "good house" as an absolute necessity if I were to survive college life. What did I have that they would value? The answer escaped me. Would "college men" (those formidable unknowns) like me? What clothes should I take on our trip? All these questions were big ones, important to me. I longed for the right answers.

Late in July, we left for Tennessee in our black Dodge sedan. It was the first long trip to be planned by car: always before, we had traveled by train. But BumBum was almost four now and enjoyed riding. She was a cheery baby and so much fun that Jimmie and I each delighted in having our own turn to amuse her, hold her, sing to her, or cuddle her warm sleeping body. We went first to cousins of my father's in St. Louis, where she made us laugh the second morning we were there by appearing in a large hat, tugging Mother's Boston Bag across the floor. "I've picked up all my things now and I'm ready to go home," she announced firmly.

How little we knew. . .

## Swing Low—I

*We were stowed away in our divinely appointed*
*places in the rear seat of the car,*
*my brother behind my father*
*who always did the night driving*
*and I back of Mother on the ladies' side,*
*the only proper arrangement.*
*After my baby sister was born*
*and given family names in the Southern style*
*she was held on Mother's lap*
*secure in her feminine sphere.*
*We didn't even know any families*
*where children sat on the front seat—*
*certainly not the Cadys in their*
*black beetle of a Model-T*
*or the McCatherines in the modish*
*blue touring Star.*
*Our Dodge sedan, built like a block,*
*"A good car in the trucking class,"*
*Daddy always said,*
*sailed down the ribbon of highway*

*sometimes reaching the furious speed*
*of 35 miles an hour.*
                    *And as we rode*
*in moonlight or shadow, rain or heat*
*or cold, my parents sang.*
*They had gone to singing school together*
*when they were young, and sang in parts,*
*Mother's clear soprano circling around*
*and over Daddy's sure tenor in*
*songs from The Golden Wreath or*
*Carmina Princetonia. Sometimes*
*it was Polly-Wolly-Doodle, sometimes*
*Juanita or The Lone Fish Ball.*
*Their repertoire seemed endless,*
*included The Mermaid, Romeo and Juliet,*
*The Mikado, Pinafore, Pirates of Penzance.*
*We had favorites and called out our requests*
*in voices that grew sleepier*
*as the miles stretched on.*
*Jimmie would ask for Rig-A-Jig-Jig and*
*I would counter with Billy-Magee-Magaw.*
*They sang on and on until their voices*
*were ready for The Birds of Spring,*
*a taxing anthem. Mother's treble soared*
        *The bi-i-i-rds of spri-i-i-ng*
*and my father affirmed*
        *Have co-o-o-me again*
*Together they commanded*
        *List to their soft sweet song*
*The notes caressed each other*
*separated*
*and joined again.*
*I shivered in anticipation of*
*each phrase. Happiness*
*made me warm all over.*
*Awake and missing nothing, I was*

*glad my brother was asleep.*
*I hugged myself in the darkness.*
*Sleep was beyond me.*
*We drew closer to home and always*
*The concert ended with spirituals:*
*Go Down, Moses; I Couldn't Hear Nobody*
*Pray, perhaps, I Know The Lord's Laid*
*His Hands On Me. When we passed the*
*cemetery, just before driving up*
*our hill, their voices swung into*
*Swing Low, Sweet Chariot.*
*Stumbling out of the car, an arm*
*around my shoulders as we went into*
*the house, I knew they had carried me home.*

## Swing Low—II

August in Tennessee left its steamy imprint on our skin. Walking downtown on the old board sidewalks, I felt threatened by the passion flower vines climbing up from the hollow, trying (I shuddered) to catch my bare legs and sandaled feet. Mama and Cousin Almira were behind us, each holding one of BumBum's small hands. My brother, Jimmie, and I led the group, on our best behavior because we were visitors and wanted to impress Daddy's cousins, Almira, Emma, and Harry. The two spinster sisters and bachelor brother were all home together for the summer, hosting our visit from Arkansas. During the school year, Almira taught at Maryville College and Harry was Professor of Latin and Greek in Memphis. Emma was the homemaker.

I was fourteen that summer, still a child in some important ways, although I had just graduated from high school and was apprehensive lest anyone think me less than a model of sophistication. My own doubts about this I tried hard to keep to myself. Jimmie was ten, dedicated, I felt, to making me miserable. His sunny good nature was in marked contrast, however, to my moodiness and talent for self-dramatization. His constant teasing was a particular thorn in my side, but it certainly kept me from taking myself too seriously.

BumBum was skipping along between her elders that summer day as if the heat mattered not at all. It mattered to me, although I had a reputation in the family for being the best able to stand high temperatures. As we went shop to shop while Mother and Almira did small errands, my head began to ache, dull throbbing pain, and my brains felt loose as though they were bumping against my skull. Jimmie was less mischievous than usual and dragged along beside me with what looked like fever flags in his fair cheeks. Mother suggested that the heat might be a little too much for us and stopped at an ice cream parlor for cold drinks. My cherry coke tasted terrible for once, and Jimmie left most of his strawberry pop in the bottle. BumBum cheerily drank her lemonade and the grownups had iced tea. We all crunched our ice and were a bit revived from the cool air stirred by big ceiling fans.

The walk home, four short blocks, seemed endless, and I fancied that the passion flowers were bigger, more rampant than before. As we entered the cool house, shades drawn against the 95 degree heat, I asked if I might go to bed. Mother looked surprised—I hated naps, was not a daytime sleeper. Jimmie almost ran to the bathroom, and when we heard sounds of retching, Mother followed him. Later, when Daddy and Cousin Harry came home from the campus where they had attended a conference of some kind, I heard Mother apologizing for our behavior to the cousins, "I can't imagine what's going on. They are usually good travelers. To cause you all that trouble—"

The matter of trouble was pooh-poohed, BumBum charmed everyone with her playfulness, and our indisposition was put down to "summer complaint." By bedtime, Jimmie's symptoms and mine were almost identical: bad headaches, stiff necks, and general gastro-intestinal problems. We both had fevers, not alarmingly high.

By morning the picture had changed dramatically. Jimmie, contrary to his usual pattern, felt fine, was hungry enough to demand and consume a huge breakfast. My head still ached but I had no other symptoms and just felt "raggy" as if something terrible had happened to me.

But Baby Keith was ill—just as we had been but more severely. Her temperature rose to frightening heights and her vomiting was ceaseless. Our cousins called their family doctor, an imposing but kindly man, who hurried over with his little black bag and bounded upstairs to the bedroom where she lay limp and impassive, unlike her usual self.

The following two days were a nightmare. Mother and Daddy were at BumBum's bed for hours at a time, spelling each other for short periods when they tried without success to rest. Cool cloths and ice packs were prepared for the small head, whose curls had been flattened by perspiration. Warm towels were wrapped around her aching arms and legs. She was SO good but her agony was evident.

Toward evening on the second day it was apparent that it was hard for her to breathe. She was propped up on pillows. The doctor returned—came downstairs shaking his head. Jimmie was outside in the hammock.

I was frightened. It was all very strange. We were not at home. Dr. Ellis could not be with us, although I knew that my father had talked with him on the telephone. Our parents had withdrawn to the bedroom upstairs; when they kissed us, we knew they were thinking of BumBum.

Shortly after midnight, I was awakened from a troubled sleep by my father who said only, "Hurry, dear. You'll want to say goodbye." He put a light blanket around me and led me to BumBum's room. She looked very small against the pillows and very tired. Jimmie stood beside Mother, who had one arm around him, the other hand cupping her baby's shoulder. Daddy's voice broke as he said, "Honey girl, you may kiss her cheek, if you want." I bent over the tiny form, felt the terrifying quiet of her chest. My father's arms tightened around me as the four of us watched the tired eyes close.

The strangeness persisted. My parents sobbed in each other's arms after they learned that they could not take BumBum home for burial—infantile paralysis was considered so virulent that permission to transport the body could not be obtained. (She had died of the form now identified as bulbar polio.) It was necessary to seal her body in a lead casket for burial. Friends of the family did what they could, but many were afraid of contagion. Food and flowers were left at the door and speedy departure followed. The house soon smelled like a combination of a church supper, a fading summer garden, and a florist's shop.

I remember little of the simple funeral service in Almira's parlor except that music was played on a cabinet organ like the one at my grandmother's in Kansas. The relentless heat faded the flowers before our eyes; their dying perfumed the still air.

At the cemetery, the smallness of the dark hole cut in the lush green grass terrified me. It looked like a trap.

How could she ever escape the sealed coffin, the narrow, close pit? The markers were all alike, I noticed, all flat in the earth. No, I felt numbly, BumBum was NOT like all the rest!

We had planned to stop on our way home from Maryville for a month in the piney woods at nearby Calderwood, an almost deserted mountain resort which had been enlarged as headquarters for the projected TVA dam. My parents decided to continue with their plans. It must have offered some comfort to them in its isolation and quiet. In many ways it reminded me of Green Mountain Falls in Colorado, where I had spent my last summer as an "only" before my brother's birth. But now in place of the laughter and high spirits I remembered from that time, I often heard weeping from my parents' bedroom—not only Mother's wounded cries but the deep groans of my father's grief. I had not known that men cried! I wept, too, as I thought of going home without Baby Keith.

The time came when we had to do just that. Cross-country driving was a real challenge then, and our square black Dodge sedan, running-boards packed tightly with suitcases, gasoline cans, and food chests, African water bag swinging from the front, carried four of us back along the roads from Tennessee to Arkansas. On the way east, there had been five.

This trip had no singing, and for months my parents' songs were stilled. The quiet deepened as we drove by the graveyard and up the hill to our lonely home. Even the streaming tears were silent.

## Night Riders

*Night riders, marching in daylight now,*
*Carry like torches placards of*
*Fear and hate. They*
*Return me to my childhood South.*
*I stand in my father's study,*
*Plead tearfully with him to join*
*The Klan, so I can sport full*
*Status with my peers, boasting,*
*"My Daddy said—*
*That Darkie was scared white—"*
*He listens quietly, does not agree,*
*Says he cannot join in what he*
*Disbelieves.  Desperate, I mention*
*Names—fathers of my friends,*
*The banker, the Sunday-school superintendent,*
*His friends—and my trump card—our*
*Family doctor, his confidant and ally.*
*Still he refuses, mentions conscience*
*(A sacred word, fellow traveler with*
*Belief) and finally says to me, "Honey,*
*Try to understand.*
*I'll never walk behind a mask."*

*Then one cool night in early autumn,*
*I stood on a low curb across from*
*Campus steps, in front of the Kappa Sig*
*House, talking and laughing with my*
*Dearest friends, waiting for the firefly*
*Pricks of light far up the avenue to become*
*The flaming torches of a real parade.*
*Four abreast, men marched, their sheeted*
*Bodies radiant from the leaping flames.*
*The peaked white hoods concealed all*
*But eyes, deep hidden in the shadows*

*Flickering across the masks. Who*
*Knew which one was hers, till Mary*
*Called "Look, there's my Daddy. See*
*Those blue pants there." And Lucy Ellen,*
*"I'd know Papa's old brown shoes just anywhere."*

*My father was not marching. I'd never have*
*To name him by his feet or trouser legs.*

*On they paraded toward East Mountain*
*Where the burning cross lit up the sky*
*And where the Methodists had just dismissed*
*Their summer conference, all souls safely saved.*

*Daddy, I knew you through your eyes and*
*Unmasked face. My questions never went*
*Unheard. I'm trying still to understand.*

*Who will be next? It's hard to know.*
*Such fires once lit, will feed on any fuel.*

## Coming of Age

I grew up in a period when speed in academic achievement was highly prized. Standardized tests were just coming into their own. Lewis Terman had brought out the Stanford/Binet test, and the term IQ (intelligence quotient), frequently misused and/or interpreted, was popular across the land. My father, who had been a friend of Terman in graduate school, enjoyed playing with his test and others and found many opportunities to experiment with various educational theories and practices. Testing was frequent and non-threatening at Peabody and we seemed to be learning quite a bit in our unconventional ways. We were quite competitive, I guess, in our small group, and a couple of us more or less hopscotched our way through the first eight grades.

My best friend/dearest enemy and I found ourselves suddenly in high school, still on the same campus. She was twelve, I was eleven, and there were differences between us. She played the piano, well; I still played football with my Hill Street friends. Mary Frances' hair was bobbed; mine still hung in long curls. Within the year she had developed a "figure;" my thin chest and hips showed no softening curves. The principal theme of her conversation began to be boys, and she was especially concerned over whether they liked her or not and whether they knew which ones she liked. It seemed pretty silly to me.

I evidently tried hard to hold up my end of our competitive relationship, however, as revealed in a letter from my Memory Book. It is from Mary Frances to me, dated August 30, 1921. We would be juniors in high school in the fall. She was visiting relatives in Oklahoma City and she starts right out with the challenging, "You certainly did write me a sweet letter. You act like I never saw or heard of a boy." This statement, written in Number Two lead pencil on folded peach stationery, is followed by ten (count them!) exclamation points.

Mary Frances goes on to describe sitting on the porch "the other night (I mean morning) at 2:00 a.m. with a gang of them" and on another night, "dancing every dance with boys until 1:00 a.m.—there sure are some cute ones down here."

Just to reinforce her seniority, she states, "I am thirteen now"—doubly underlined with five exclamation points. Mary Frances further emphasizes my junior standing by writing that if I had any dates at all, she is sure they were in the afternoon. "Most of mine," she brags, "have lasted until morning." A total of twenty-eight of the useful and appropriate punctuation marks attend this demeaning (to me) comparison. She closes with, "Yours until you have as many dates at night as I have," hammering down the hatches with the under-lined postscript message of spurious sympathy, "I hope I haven't made you feel bad." What would we do without best friends to keep us humble? I only wish that I could find some of my letters from that summer. If ever a challenge to fictionalize experience existed, it lay in our earnest efforts at one-upmanship.

Classes in high school were fun, but I was confused in P.E., a whole period to spend on playing games, running, even folk dancing. We changed into full black bloomers and white middies, put on tennis shoes and socks. What a treat—and yet there were always some girls who didn't change, who sat on the sidelines after calling out "Regular" at roll call and then kept score or were dismissed to the library or even lay down on the couch in the teacher's office. What was going on? I finally asked one of my older classmates what she meant when she answered "Regular." She looked at me a minute with unbelieving eyes, shook her head and replied, "Oh, I just fell off the roof."

How awful, I thought, it must have really hurt. I knew what it felt like to jump from a height. But when I tried to sympathize with her, she put me off with, "You're so dumb! Grow up!" and flounced off laughing to her friends.

I learned in time, when Mary Frances confided proudly to me that her "periods" had started, what "Regular" meant and that "falling off the roof" was the current vernacular, but none of this seemed to apply to me. To ask my fastidious mother about such personal matters would have been impossible. Even when she had abruptly terminated my football career by implying that I would someday feel less like a boy, the conversation went no further. When, oh when, would I be able to hold my own in P.E. by answering "Regular" like everyone else in monthly turn?

Finally, of course, the day came when, after what I had assumed was a more severe stomach ache than most and oddly displaced, I found the telltale bright spots of blood on my panties. Strangely awed by the fact that some dramatic change in my body had at last occurred, I overcame my reluctance to impose on my mother's privacy and went to her room. She put her arms around me and, to my surprise, began to initiate me carefully and explicitly into what she knew of feminine hygiene. From the big linen closet she brought out a package of intricately cut birdseye napkins, showed me how to fold them so that tabs front and back could be pinned to a garter-belt-like contraption that went around my waist, holding the thick folded pad tight between my legs. I felt as though I were being fitted with harness.

Then she took me to the downstairs bathroom, where she filled the white enameled diaper pail, just retired by my baby sister, with cold water from the faucet and instructed me in the facts of soaking and rinsing, washing and rinsing again. "Every woman must learn to take care of herself, neatly and quietly, with the utmost cleanliness and privacy." She asked if I had any pain, suggested that I lie down for awhile, and then she brought me a hot water bottle, stroked my hair and gave me a kiss.

That had been the extent of my sex education when I entered college, the U of A, at age fourteen. Mary Frances and I had been the subjects of some newspaper stories about "precocious freshmen," had gone through sorority rushing and had happily pledged to different houses. A few unpleasant implications about "faculty brats who'll raise grade point averages" as the motive for our desirability had reached my ears, but I was too pleased to really be in college to pay much attention. Mother and Daddy had hoped that I would take a year off between high school and college, work on my French and music and, most of all, grow a year older. But staying with my class was of paramount importance to me and so I forged naively ahead.

I did find myself one day in the college auditorium, where with all my sister freshmen I was to hear a talk about SEX. It was about time, I thought, and there were lots of things I wanted to know. But the speaker immediately raised my doubts. Thin and fluttery, of a most uncertain age, she spoke in a whistling whisper about "virginity" and the many attacks made on that priceless virtue by demanding, promiscuous men. What they did and where and how were not specified, but the monsters she described bore no resemblance to my father and his friends nor to the somewhat callow youths I had known in high school and hoped to meet on campus. "Petting" she seemed to call "handling" and we were sternly warned against any such intimacies, since they would lead inevitably to immediate loss of that priceless pearl, "virginity." Again she did not say how, but with a monstrous leap of logic stated conclusively that one should always welcome one's menstrual period as a triumph of preservation—"The rejoicing time!" She rose to full voice. "One's virginity has been kept intact!"

Although there were subdued giggles, round and about, we were too thoroughly embarrassed to do more than shuffle quietly out, pink-cheeked and shamed—for her and for ourselves. She was a fool, we thought, but what about all those men intent on robbing us of virtue and good name?

My older sorority sisters, appalled to find out how truly ignorant I was, initiated some social rules for me that I would never have accepted from my family. I was to go out on no single dates for the first quarter, only double dates for me and preferably with a sophomore or upper classman. Blind dates could be chosen by an older "sister." They took on their chaperonage with surprisingly good grace, and I went right along with it, failing to recognize that not all freshman pledges were handled so carefully. I only hoped that Mary Frances never heard about it. But she was across town in the Chi Omega house. It worked well until the night I went out with Alice and her steady boy friend, who had brought along a fraternity brother for me.

Jake Cummings was a junior transfer from the University of Alabama. Tall, sandy, a golfer of skill, with a convincing "line" that predicted his later success as an attorney, he had become a BMOC (big man on campus) already. Why he should want to date me was a flattering mystery. He paid me headturning attention, turned on his charm at once, "loved my eyes," and when he casually put his arm over the back of my seat at the movies and later reached for my hand, I couldn't believe this was actually happening. My hand tingled in his. We had sundaes after the show and then Jake and I climbed into the back seat of Alice's boy friend's car to go back to the house. We took the long way, and when Alice turned and said to me, "We still have some time before curfew. We're going to park awhile," Jake pulled me over to him. He was an experienced and insistent young man. My delight at having attracted him changed to alarm as his busy hands seemed to be everywhere at once. Holding me close with one arm, he used his free hand to caress my breasts; smothering my protests with kisses, he began to unbutton my dress. Alice and Bill were off in a world alone in the front seat. Happy little moans and gurgles drifted back to us. I had wanted to appear knowing and experienced, but Jake's enthusiastic assault began to frighten me. I had petted before but this was different. Pulling up my skirt, he unhooked one stocking from my garter belt, pulled down my panties. I was fighting now, desperately but quietly. My mind raced. What did one do in a case like this? Is this what the fluttery lady was talking about? How exactly did one lose one's virginity? Had I lost mine?

Jake's hands stroked and prodded. He had put one leg across me to hold me down on the seat. I felt a finger thrust between the labia as he held my face down with his dreadful kisses. I bit his tongue. "God damn you!" He straightened up. I pulled away, trying to rearrange my clothes. Bill and Alice drew apart. The car started. Jake was angrily wiping his mouth with a bloody handkerchief. The bite was not deep, I guess, but it had been effective. He furiously left me alone.

When we reached the house, I jumped out of the car and ran in without a word. Alice found me later, crying in the bathroom as I showered and showered. She demanded the story. "What a louse! You poor kid—well, anyway it's a story he'll never tell on himself with that sore tongue. I'm awfully sorry, honey, that guy's a beast." She gave me a quick hug and hurried off to bed.

But it wasn't over for me. Truly ignorant and full of fear, remembering that intruding finger thrust, I was panic stricken. Could I have become pregnant, I wondered. Was that how it happened? I flew to the library the next morning, found the anatomy section, pulled *Gray's Anatomy* and some other heavy volumes and pored over sketch after sketch of female anatomy. In 1923, libraries were not exactly crowded with books on sex education and intercourse. I could not find any explicit statement either to confirm or refute my fears. How awful if I were to have a baby in this ugly, ugly way. My parents had given me such trust. I had truly valued myself. Could just this awful handling make me pregnant?

Head aching with questions, I left the library after carefully re-shelving the books so that no one would know what I had been seeking. What could I do? How could I find out? Dr. Ellis would surely tell my parents, would be equally disappointed in me. Mother? I could never, ever ask her such a private question, describe to her how soiled, how dirty I felt by being touched in such a hungry way. She was so clean, so private, so remote from such things. How had she ever had me? Or Jimmie? Or Baby Keith? And Mother was so sad these days, so grieved over the death of her youngest child, our elfin Keith, who had been left in Tennessee. All of us tried hard to spare her, to help her laugh with us again. How could I burden, sadden her with this awful tale?

It took me almost ten days to get an answer. I cut most of my classes, asked permission to go home for a week from the house, told my family I was tired and needed a rest. Most of my time was spent walking or bathing. I still felt dirty.

At last I went to the safest person I knew: my father. We were much alike, had always known a special bond. And he was always honest with me. What he told me, I knew would be true. So I went to his office on campus, told Miss Lano, his secretary, that I needed to see him alone. If he was busy, I would wait. And in a matter of half an hour or so (he had been talking with another faculty member) I was in his office. One look at me and he said, "I'll be busy the rest of the afternoon, Miss Lano. Please handle any calls."

The door closed and he took my hand. I talked and cried, alternately and at the same time. The relief of being with him and sharing my enormous fear was so great that sometimes I just sat with my hand in his and let the tears run down my cheeks. He questioned me very gently, never encroaching on what dignity I was trying to salvage. "Only his hands?" he asked. Then, "My poor dear girl—"

Quickly, he reassured me. There was no danger of pregnancy, none whatsoever. And then followed a rapid description of what intercourse was and could be between loving men and women. Angered as he obviously was over the misadventure, he did not dirty it further. To my amazement then and clearer understanding now that I am a parent myself, he frequently seemed to feel responsible in some way for my ignorant fears. "You have learned so quickly, dear," he comforted me. "You seem in some ways to have grown up so fast. We have been wrong in assuming what you knew about men and women. Not all men are like the young man who frightened you so badly. You are attractive, very attractive, and some young men feel that girls are to be hunted. He would have been proud of his conquest—and he gave no thought to how you might feel. After all, you scarcely knew each other." He went on to give me some very sound advice and most of all, he rebuilt my confidence in men and in men and women together.

"I love your mother very much—as you know," he went on. "When I kiss her, hug her, pat or stroke her, my hands are saying that to her. That message is very different from hands that say, 'See, I've gotten in! I'm playing in private, forbidden territory—' You were very right to fight them away. Be sure what your body is saying. It should be at ease with what it is doing." I began to understand how my intensely private mother could have had me and my brother and sister. It couldn't have been easy for him and for my mother to have a child so quick to learn in some ways and so deeply and unexpectedly uninformed in others.

But with his help, I was coming of age. My father's arms were around me. I sobbed quietly on his shoulder.

Somehow I felt clean again. "Let's walk home," he said. "Would you like to wash your face? I'll wait for you downstairs."

## Treading Collegiate Waters

To be a college freshman at the University of Arkansas in the 1920's was a real challenge. Lest our lowly status be forgotten for a moment, we all wore green felt arm-bands with an appliqued small white "beanie." Frosh men wore similar green beanies, pushed far back, dipping over one eye or ruler straight on the head, depending on the personal style of the wearer. Freshman girls wore many tiny green bows in their hair, the total effect tending toward a pickaninny look. We were reported to the Student Discipline Committee for infractions and I forget what dire penalties were imposed. I certainly was too fearful to risk much infringement of rules.

Fear played a large role in my first year at the University, strangely so since I was a faculty brat and had lived on or near the campus since I was five. My only schooling had been at Peabody, on campus. Perhaps this very proximity provoked my qualms. I had always looked on my father's college students as superbeings, images to emulate from a distance. Now I was one of them—and yet not really one of them. My difference in age had been seized upon by the press for news stories about me as the youngest student to enter college in the autumn of '23. I had even received letters from clipping bureaus, enclosing clippings and soliciting my trade! This publicity embarrassed and almost shamed me.

Mother and Daddy helped by teasing gently and laughing over my sudden notoriety.

Probably the stories helped my position in rushing and I became a "nugget," heavily rushed by all the sororities on campus. This was before preferential bidding and the approved technique was simply to besiege a rushee with pleas, offers, claims to campus glamor and fame, even tears, until the exhausted girl said "Yes" out of fatigue, despair or, hopefully, desire. Still numbed by the death of my baby sister in August, I found such powerhouse tactics all but impossible to bear and pledged my future to the one sorority whose members had had the sensitivity to give me a little space—offer a bid and then leave me alone for awhile to think it over. It was a good choice and my older sorority sisters did a great deal to help me catch up and keep up with college life. It was good for me, too, to have chosen a house for myself rather than going along with Mary Frances and Betty to another group, one founded on the University of Arkansas campus and, understandably, the largest and most popular.

Classes were not as comfortable as they had been in high school. Larger and infinitely more formal, they made different demands. In chemistry lecture we sat in a circular amphitheater rising around the imposing lab table where demonstrations were performed. More than one hundred students answered a formal roll call until seats were assigned and monitors could easily check attendance while the lecture progressed. I was so terrified that when the roll call got down to the "J's" and "Margaret Jewell" boomed out, only a pitiful squeak of "Present" came out of my trembling lips.

Chemistry lab was even more frightening—in a different way. The tubes and beakers and Bunsen burners dismayed me, the odors offended me, and stains seemed always on my hands. Finally, my worst fears seemed realized when the wood distillation setup of my facing desk partner blew up and a piece of glass skimmed by my cheek, drawing blood as it went its way. It took a tremendous amount of persuasion from Professor Humphrey and the fact that he was impossibly handsome to get me to continue chemistry.

Happily, all college life was not in the classroom or laboratory. On Thanksgiving, the whole family went down to Fort Smith on a special train for the big game with Oklahoma A & M (of which my former debate partner's father, Dr. Bradford Knapp, was now president. I saw Marion across the field, madly waving her pompon). It rained heavily throughout the game and spectators had the unique experience of seeing a future senator, "Bill" Fulbright, as he was known on campus, make ten yards sitting down as he skidded forward in the mud, ball clutched to his soaked jersey. Thrilled with my parents' extraordinary generosity, I failed to realize for years how much easier it must have been to face this first holiday without BumBum in a festive setting away from home.

It continued to rain that year. Hill Street, which was unpaved like many of the Fayetteville streets, became impassable and our trusty Dodge sedan stayed in the garage for some time. The general dreariness continued past Christmas and deepened our grief as we tried to celebrate without our beloved small sister.

Spring finally came, which I celebrated in my own fashion, nourishing an enormous crush on a tall handsome football player, Norman Hastings. He was twice my size and several years my senior but he was kind to me, bought me cherry cokes at Tony's in Shuler Town by the station and he seemed often to be headed toward my father's campus office. It finally dawned on me that he was inventing excuses to see Miss Lano, Daddy's secretary, she of the beautiful hands. She must have been all of twenty-three or twenty-four and seemed much too old to me to hold any romantic interest. How wrong I was!

That spring was memorable in other ways, however, and was incredibly beautiful because of the winter rains. All the flowering trees came into blossom, and the bulbs—tulips, jonquils, lilies, narcissus, hyacinths—were blooming in profusion in early April when I was initiated into Pi Beta Phi. Mrs. Nickerson, the Grand Vice-President, was in Fayetteville on an inspection visit and she conducted the ritual. A tall, deep-bosomed woman of stately bearing, with a crown of firmly waved gray hair and an omnipresent strand of heavy pearls swinging to her waist, she had awed all of us with her very presence. When my turn came to be presented for initiation and my blindfold was removed, I was totally overwhelmed by the vision of this imposing woman seated at the end of an aisle of white-robed, candlebearing sisters. Instantly, I dropped to my knees—the only appropriate gesture, I felt, for such nobility. Efforts by my escorts to get me up on my feet were strenuous and eventually enabled me to move forward and kneel again at my vision's feet. At last, I had survived my freshman year. I was truly a college woman. I was now fifteen!

That summer my father accepted a speaking tour in the Pacific Northwest, suggested to him for a good many years. First promoted by Dr. A. A. Cleveland of Washington State College, a dear friend since their graduate days at Clark University, the tour snowballed as other colleges, universities, and teachers' institutes learned that Daddy would be available. It was almost a year since BumBum's death; he was eager to provide a change of scene for my mother.

And so we embarked on what we felt was real adventure—a summer in the Far West. It was to change our lives in ways we could not imagine. A cottage in Seaside, Oregon was rented, close by the summer home the Clevelands had enjoyed for years. Mother, Jimmie, and I would take up residence there. Daddy would join us on weekends and whenever he could steal away from his demanding schedule. We excitedly planned wardrobes for a different climate.

The very real difference between the Oregon beaches and the hot Ozark summer, however, was something I didn't clearly realize or chose to ignore. A July-August wardrobe for me seemed to demand organdy and dotted swiss, linen, voile, possibly shantung. In vain, my mother tried to persuade me of the need for heavier clothes. I was as unyielding as I knew how to be. We stood toe-to-toe in argument until my exasperated mother finally said, "Very well, Margaret. We can't go on this way or we'll never get to Oregon. I will choose one complete outfit for you. You may pack whatever else you wish."

And it was done. Mother chose a soft coral sweater and skirt, a blouse, a scarf, and then I scornfully piled in my Southern ruffles. Needless to say, I came close to freezing in Seaside until I resentfully donned the skirt and sweater; it was almost threadbare by the end of the summer.

The Far West lived up to our expectations in unexpected ways. Our train west was delayed by forest fires as it made its way through Montana. The whole state seemed to our eyes to be ablaze or blackened in the aftermath of the firestorm. Smoking tree trunks reached against the sky, fallen timbers lay close to the tracks, sullen coals still smoldering in their ashes. Thinking of the cool green Ozark forests, dampened by summer thunderstorms as well as gentle rains, we looked with horror at this devastation.

When we reached Seaside, an even stranger sight confronted us. Stretched to dry on the side of a woodhouse next door to our cottage was a fresh black bear skin. Its actual dimensions I don't know, but it looked to us far larger than even the Paul Bunyan estimates of animal size. It would have put Babe, the Blue Ox, to shame. So this was the Wild West!

I tried ocean bathing and found the famed Japanese Current to be just one degree above actual freezing rather than the comfortable bathtub warmth I had expected. Purple with cold, teeth chattering, barely able to walk out of the surf, I eventually joined family and friends in the heated saltwater natatorium on the boardwalk. My life had been saved! Later in the summer, I was to record my all-time swimming achievement: 120 feet in that warm, sustaining water, using, of course, my reliable sidestroke.

Labor Day found us on a windy corner of Market Street, watching a really remarkable display of San Francisco's work force. I had refused to wear my sweater and skirt one more day (after all, I was in California!) and was shivering in a thin pongee. My parents held their tongues, hoping, I'm sure, that I'd somehow survive my stubbornness.

I did survive, at least long enough to sail on the *Harvard* for the overnight trip to Los Angeles. That long forgotten custom of festive marine travel back and forth between San Francisco and Los Angeles on what I think was called the Yale/Harvard Line is a sad loss to economy and changing times. The abundant food, throbbing music ("Melancholy Baby," "Hard Hearted Hannah," "Toot, Toot, Tootsie") and general gaiety made me feel like a genuine world traveler.

And it was in this somewhat jaded mood that I looked forward to meeting De Witt Williams again. De Witt and I had ruled as King and Queen of the Homecoming celebration in Emporia, Kansas when I was just past my fourth birthday. He was of equal age. Our float was drawn by students who had chosen this means to honor our professor fathers: James Ralph Jewell and Pelagius Williams. Before that year was out, my family had moved to the Ozarks, and sometime later his family's move was to Eagle Rock, California. We were set for an unlikely reunion. After the first awkwardness, it went well. We found that we could laugh over our brief excursion into royal living some twelve years before. His tales of Hollywood and the motion picture studios enthralled me; my southern drawl (deepened for the occasion) seemed to hold him spellbound. After lunch with the two families, we parted, vowing to write forever and to see each other again as soon as possible. After a couple of letters apiece, this vow faded. Who first forgot to write, I can't remember.

The sheer, gaping drama of the Grand Canyon put Los Angeles out of my mind. It was impossible, I thought, for the earth to split so far beneath its surface without falling apart. Shuddering, I looked around with apprehension, listening for the first crack. At least my family and I were on the same side!

Next day, riding on mule back down Bright Angel Trail into the canyon and on to the Colorado, cutting its way deeper into the earth by the minute, I had a different set of fears. The canyon rim outlined against the sky, so far above us, looked as though it might close against the opposite rim at any moment, healing its wound and trapping the unwary, such as myself, who had ventured into the very bowels of the earth. Much as I enjoyed sunning myself and eating a hearty lunch on the river bank, I was relieved when the guide called us together for the return climb. On the way down, he had chatted in a folksy way with his string of mules and riders. "Let go his reins, mister," he called to a nervous bankerly man trying hard to pull his mule away from a point where both the beast's head and his rump overhung the vast depths of the canyon. "That critter cares more for his life than you do!"

He was quieter now and tired, as were his mules and their riders. Pulling at his bushy handlebar moustache and spitting expertly down to the Colorado, he did manage a response to a portly middle-aged woman, obviously no rider, who had voiced frequent complaints throughout the trip. Her latest lament was of chafing and how sore she had become after hours in the saddle. "Don't worry, ma'am," he spat out. "Them sore places'll heal over tough." Riders chuckled, the complainer turned a deep crimson. We plodded up the narrow trail in silence.

It was good to be home again and even the cold waters of the Pacific seemed more acceptable as I shared tales of the summer with my friends. Sophomore year had to be better than the first; after all, I knew what to expect. A pair of elbow length black kid gloves for my sixteenth birthday gave promise of dances and parties to come. But, in fact, my sophomore year turned out to be more of a holding operation, sort of like treading water to keep from going under. I went to a modest number of fraternity dances and big all-college balls. I hiked miles on Sunday afternoons with a mixed group of friends over the nearby hills, through hickory and chinquapin trees. We ate all we could of small pumpkin-shaped persimmons, showing by their mauve overtint that they had been frost-bitten and were ready, and brought the rest of our booty back to Ruth's, from whose home we had started. There we had hot chocolate or bowls of steaming soup, nodding wearily, eager to go home for a hot bath and bed. Woe betide those who had left homework to do before Monday morning.

Ruth had become my dearest friend since her arrival in Fayetteville. Her father had left the University of Illinois to become head of the geology department at the University of Arkansas, and it was he who had introduced me to the Ozark caves. The competitive aspects of my long friendship with Mary Frances had become too much for me to handle, and we had fortunately pledged different houses. We rarely saw each other in college except by happenstance. But Ruth and I rode together in the early mornings, the hot noontimes, and on midnight trails under a full moon, stopping for huge country breakfasts at the Green Tree Inn, out east of town.

Frequently, we packed small lunches and counted on fruit purchased or pilfered from some roadside farm. We became expert at balancing a small watermelon between our hips and the saddlehorn, although once in awhile the round green ball would roll away and crash down on the trail. Then we'd salvage what pieces we could and munch on the ripe red sweetness, juice running down from our laughing mouths. We had time to talk about everything in the world, and there was adventure, too.

One fine day we ventured farther than usual on a brush-hidden mountain trail and rode into a working still. It was prohibition time and the mountain people could make far more money producing White Lightning from their corn than by selling it through legitimate channels.

"Federal men" were, of course, on constant lookout for such operations that the mountaineers guarded vigilantly. We had hardly had a chance to take in the red-coaled stone fire box and the shining copper coils before three mountain men in dark pants, faded shirts and loose, unbuttoned vests surrounded us. They all carried shotguns which they trained on us with level-eyed questioning stares. No one said anything. Then Ruth and I burst out together like a trained chorus, "We're lost! Could you gentlemen tell us how to get back to Fayetteville?"

"Fay't'ville, hunh," the youngest man grunted and glanced sideways at his fellows.

"Oh, yes, please. We don't want to frighten our folks by staying out any longer."

It worked. Gun in hand but barrel pointing down, the still-keeper directed us down a steep hillside, roughly the way we had come, and pointed toward a dusty road in the distance. "I reckon you'd best not follow a trail," he advised. As we crashed downhill through bushes and small trees, even our horses seemed to know enough to move fast and not look back. It was sometime before we shared this tale with our families, and we definitely did not need their admonition not to try to find our way back.

Because of our close friendship, I had always assumed that Ruth would follow me into the sorority I had chosen and I saw to it that her name was prominent on our rush list. I made much of her assets: good grades, good family (father on the faculty), much more popular than I, a dancer, a championship swimmer. The traits that I valued so much were somehow hard to define: a wholesome tolerance, an enthusiasm for causes, a great sense of humor, and an ability to have fun in whatever she was doing. As rush opened, however, and bidding began, I ran into unexpected opposition. "We're on top of the scholarship list now. We sure enough don't need any more brains!" came from LaRita, a campus toast who always slid by but wasted little time on study.

"Who's going to take geology, anyhow?" asked Darlene.

"I wonder what boys see in her. She's not that pretty," was the considered opinion of Mattalou Curl, the house beauty.

As a lowly sophomore, I had little influence in sorority politics. I fought loyally and then bitterly for my friend, but Ruth was blackballed. My despair over what I had learned in the campaign was great. Torn between my close friend and my new peer group, I was distraught. The next fall when Ruth was one of the Homecoming Court, I couldn't resist remarking on how great it would be if we could claim her as a member. By then I had learned what seemed to count most in rushing assets.

Our family, too, was having a difficult year—in Kansas, Grandpa and Grandma were each critically ill. My father made several trips up to Moran where they lived, Aunt Lucy (the widow of Daddy's foster brother) in faithful attendance. On one of those visits, he was called home by telegram. Jimmie had had a bad fall in the school yard, had suffered a skull fracture and a concussion. There were long, anxious days until everyone improved and we could get on with living.

Spring came and in early summer I was invited to a week-long houseparty at Marguerite's. She lived in St. Paul, up in the Ozarks, and we anticipated a week of solid fun and great food. Her mother was a notable cook. Ruth and Maxine went without me! At the last minute, I came down with mumps—very lightly and on one side only but more than enough to keep me home. I, who was never ill! A kid's disease! For two weeks I sulked in my room, reading my only solace.

A more picturesque infirmity forced me to start my junior year with my arm in a sling, the result of an insect sting or bite which occasioned a dramatic reaction. This I could make the most of in conversation, and I remember going through rush with an assumed air of great self-sacrifice. But the arm healed fairly quickly

and I was forced to face my position as an upper classman with a little more poise than I had shown before.
The happy event that really made my last two years so
special for me was that I fell in love.

Charles Federson came from Jonesboro, over by the
river across from Memphis, where his father was a
lawyer. He was neatly taller than I, dark, good looking,
and deeply tanned from the summer sun when I met
him at a house dance the Kappa Sigs held to introduce
their new pledge class. Chuck had been an Eagle Scout
and had attended the International Scout Jamboree in
Copenhagen the year before. He gave me a picture of
himself in breechclout and feathered headdress, dancing an American Indian ritual for the Jamboree. As it
said under his later picture in the annual: "The boy with
the artist's form."

I could hardly believe my good fortune. He was handsome, popular, good natured, kind. He had traveled—
the first of my peers to have left the country. And he
liked ME! I was in transports. We truly liked doing the
same things. We enjoyed talking, talking, talking. I was
able to tell him things that before I had kept only for
Ruth. And that bothered me in a way. There wasn't time
enough, I felt, for old loyalties and new love.

Charles was at the house a lot. Mother and Daddy
liked him, and the feeling of ease and approval was mutual. When Daddy was in Jonesboro for a speaking engagement, Judge Federson took him to their home for
dinner and to meet Mrs. Federson. I could hardly wait
for Charles to be initiated so that I could sport his pin.
We went on long walks, to dances and movies, had library dates (for which I managed to be suspended for a
week because of "insistent talking"). It was a wonderful
year!

Charles' attention gave me the beginnings of a self
confidence I had needed so much. Everything looked bet-

ter, seemed easier. I was chosen a Homecoming Princess and enjoyed the prestige even more because Ruth was also in the court. Bids came in for honorary organizations: Psi Chi (psychology), Kappa Delta Pi (education), and the highly regarded Lambda Tau (English and writing). The most prized invitation, however, was to the Rootin' Rubes, officially designated "the girls' pep squad," the women's branch of the Arkansas Boosters Club. Dressed in red sweaters with white felt razorbacks emblazoned upon our breasts and white pleated skirts, we served a dual purpose as goodwill ambassadors and impromptu cheer leaders. The "perks" were many and our prestige was great. We attended most out-of-town games, we had special seats in a special section, we had a chance to meet the opposing team members (although our loyalty was firmly bonded, past, present, and future to the U of A). We felt important and necessary and had unbelievable fun.

Charles was a track man, running the 440 and winning most of the time. I spent what hours I could, sitting on the same bleachers I had scorned in earlier years, watching him run.

As I remember, only one untoward incident marred the year. A family drive to Fort Smith, seventy miles away over the mountains, came to a disastrous end when the steering gear broke and my father found the wheel loose and unresponsive in his hands. Fortunately, the curve we were rounding turned in rather than out. Daddy used the brake as gently as possible, and we ran into the mountain wall instead of going off the cliff. The car was badly damaged, and we were shaken, but we were neither cut nor seriously hurt. Passersby rescued us and took us on to Fort Smith. A wrecker went back for the car. The accident made a lively conversation piece.

Later that summer, Mother enrolled for two courses in summer school: Contemporary American Novel and

Nineteenth Century English Literature. She was an excellent student and worked hard, reading and writing endless critiques. She had wanted to do this for years and now had the time she felt she needed for it. I was delegated homemaker and with Mrs. Donnelly's help kept food on the table and fresh flowers in the house. It was fun to play "turnabout."

My brother went to Scout camp that summer for twice the usual two weeks. Dreadfully homesick at first, he soon adapted and wanted to stay on and on. We drove up in mid-stay to see him and take some homecooked goodies for gustatory pleasure and morale. Fording a crystalline mountain stream, my father discovered the water far deeper than it appeared. As water rose above the floorboards of our faithful Dodge, the flooded engine sputtered and died. We were marooned in midstream.

Rolling up his pants legs, Daddy got out to reconnoiter and find the best route for Mother and me to cross the rapid water. Shoes and stockings in hand, skirts held protectively above our knees, we were soon on the bank nearest camp. A short walk and we reached our destination. Men with a sturdy truck pulled our car out of the river, and it was left on the bank to drain and dry. We were invited to join the campers overnight, and the whole experience became a great adventure. The next morning Mother and I were driven back to Fayetteville in a camp truck headed into town for provisions. Daddy stayed to drive our car back home, when and if it was dry enough to start. Someone seeing only two of us return home in a strange truck started the rumor that my father had been kidnapped, and by the time he got home, very late in the day, our phone was ringing constantly with earnest queries about our well-being and offers of every kind of help. Glad as I was that my father was safe, I couldn't help fantasizing about the romantic possibilities if he had *really* been kidnapped.

We all, including the Dodge, survived to drive up to Illinois in August, visiting our St. Louis cousins en route. A visit with the Cady's in Urbana reunited me with Ruth, who had gone to the University of Illinois with her family midyear when Dr. Cady returned to his former position there. We talked nonstop until Mother herded us all into the car for Chicago. Actually, for some reason (car trouble, probably) we had to spend the night in Cicero—at that point in the world's history the home and headquarters of Al Capone and his gang. My eager imagination went to work on that fact, and after a sleepless night of watching and waiting for the sound of gunfire, I was almost disappointed to drive out of town unscathed!

Later that week, we received word of my Grand-father's death in Moran. Daddy had visited Grandpa early in the month and knew how tenuous a grip he had on life, but the acutality of death came as a shock. It was decided that Daddy would go alone to Kansas, leaving the three of us in Chicago, and he hurriedly made the necessary train reservations. After the funeral, he rejoined us for a couple of days before going on to a tour of teachers' institutes in Indiana, an engagement of long standing. I marvel now at the relentless self-discipline my father employed to supplement his meager salary at the University.

Mother and Jimmie and I then drove to Moran to stay with Grandma and do what we could to ease her grief. It was very strange there without the slender, erect figure of my grandfather, handsome even in illness and old age, the unmistakable head of the family. Grandma seemed older and very frail, her ready wit and laughter almost absent.

When our family all returned to Fayetteville, the rush of school registration was upon us. For academic families, the New Year starts in September. It was years before I could understand what people meant when they talked about a New Year's Day that followed shortly after Christmas. Daddy, of course, was hard at work on campus; I was engulfed in pre-class rushing activities—my style considerably cramped when the Dodge, full of rushees, was broadsided by an old Essex. No one was really hurt, however, and it made for wonderful high-pitched tales of near-disaster, "He just drove that old car right into us!"

Classes got underway and I was assigned my first practice teaching. At seventeen, I was not a great deal older than my seventh grade class, but I learned how much I loved to teach (a devotion that lasts to this day) and I still have some of the prized letters of thanks from my former students.

Football season was even more exciting than usual because the Rootin' Rubes traveled with the team to several out-of-town games. We had a glorious time in Little Rock at the Hendrix game, winning a hard fought battle 14-7. But in Shreveport for the annual match with LSU, I got more than I bargained for. Trying to leave the stadium in a mob of celebrating spectators, I was hit on the head by a flying Coke bottle and lost consciousness for long enough to slip to the ground. My frantic escorts tried to stop the crowds long enough to pull me up from underfoot. They finally made it and managed to get me up and out to a car. Aside from an egg-sized lump on the head and dusty footprints on my white skirt, I was sound of wind and limb. The footprints, however, were indicative of some remarkable bruises underneath! We all decided that the less my parents and the authorities knew of this, the better, so we swore ourselves to secrecy. All went well until a week later when I tried to spirit my soiled skirt out of my closet for cleaning and ran into my mother on the stairway. Questions led to confession and the truth was out. She was horrified but, seeing me alive and well, took it better than I had expected.

Our lives were brightened that fall when Grandma came down for her first visit to our Arkansas home. She had never felt that she could leave Grandpa, whose failing health had made travel impossible. Her spirits had risen remarkably, lifted by her unfailing and unshaken faith, and she loved seeing all the places we had described to her. How we hated to see her go.

But Christmas was upon us and we celebrated with the customary large tree in the library. This year's tree was remarkable because it was a "found" tree—the product of the whole family's enterprise. Cedars, favored for Christmas, had been almost completely wiped out of the nearby hills by order of the United States Department of Agriculture because of a type of rust affecting the wide-flung apple orchards. In an intricate two-year cycle, the fungus found a host every other year in the forest and domestic cedars. All cedars were ordered cut and burned. What would we do at Christmas time?

Jimmie and a friend took it upon themselves to solve that problem. Hatchets in hand, they set out to find a waiting cedar that had somehow escaped destruction. And find one they did—about four miles out of town hidden among other larger trees on a gentle rise overlooking an abandoned farmhouse. They cut it down with their handaxes, and after considerable effort dragged it down the hill, where it fell into a deep gully beside the road. It was cold and early dark was closing in on them. They headed for home with a great tale but no tree.

Hearing the story at the dinner table, I decided that they were merely fainthearted or, worse still, had manufactured the whole saga. So the next morning, after getting directions from Jimmie and telling my parents that

*I* was going to bring home the tree, I set forth on my mission. The cold was sharpened by thin sleet that stung my face as I strode along, but soon the miles had been covered and there lay the tree, heavily decorated with mud and ice, at the bottom of a six-foot ditch. It was a big tree. After tugging and trying to lift it, I knew that I had to have help. Clapping my freezing hands together, I half-ran, half-shambled down the road toward home. And about a third of the way there, I was cheered and not really surprised to see Daddy at the wheel of our old black sedan. Jimmie was with him, and they had ropes and a canvas tarpaulin. Returning to our booty, we rolled the tree onto the tarp and managed to pull it out of its resting place. Then we hoisted it onto the top of the car, tied it firmly and carried it triumphantly home. Once there, we hosed it down, carefully washing out the considerable mud it had accumulated in its travels. Thin ice formed on the cedar fronds as we set it up beside the smokehouse to drain and hurried inside before icicles formed on us. That was a Christmas to remember.

Genuine excitement waited for me after the holidays. To my delighted surprise, I had been chosen Basketball Queen by our championship-bound team and was looking forward to a gala time when Arkansas played Baylor University in a special Basketball Homecoming, the final game of the season. My dreams were snuffed out by a tragedy of massive proportions. Coming home from their last game before ours, a bus carrying the Baylor team was involved in a terrible accident. Ten Baylor players lost their lives. The entire Southwest Conference went into mourning, and the Arkansas season ended as abruptly as had Baylor's.

My senior year rushed on. Having found out what college was all about aside from classes, I was determined to miss no part of it. Charles and I were a steady twosome, and his membership in TNE, a sub-rosa fraternity prominent then on college campuses, prompted some off-beat adventures, exciting because we often risked disciplinary action if apprehended. Our escapades were harmless but often ill-chosen in terms of safety. I particularly remember being lifted up to the bottom of a spidery fire escape on the tower of Old Main. There I removed the rope around my waist and tied it to the bottom rung of the metal ladder so that Charles and another TNE could join me—with its help. We scaled the four-story tower, climbed through an unlocked museum window, left a TNE greeting in the hands of a skeleton there and went back down the way we had come. Why? You have to be that age at that moment to know the answer!

Somehow, I had come into modest prominence in campus organizations. Becoming a member of Blackfriars, the honorary dramatic ensemble, meant a great deal to me and was lots of fun. I held offices in the Rubes and in Lambda Tau and had been elected president of Kappa Delta Pi and Psi Chi. But the honor that probably meant most to me was being named chapter president of my sorority. It had been a long, bumpy road from the frightened freshman pledge of 1923 to that expression of confidence from my peers in 1927.

When I was elected president of the recently formed Women's League of the university and sent as a delegate to the national conference at the University of Illinois, my cup really ran over. Under my picture in the Who's Who in American Colleges section of the *Razorback* ran the tongue-in-cheek statement beside my list of affiliations, "She just won't be a mere member!"

The Illinois conference was a wonder and a delight to me. I was able to stay with Ruth and so had a great reunion, catching up on all the things we hadn't put in letters. I met interesting college women from all over the country, many expressing strongly feminist views that had never occurred to me. I had always simply enjoyed being a girl/woman and, while recognizing the differences and appeal of the other sex, let it go at that.

And here on the Illinois campus I suddenly found that by some strange magic I knew how to attract and deal with that other sex. It was intoxicating! I made two conquests while I was there that lasted over years and miles through correspondence, although our hopes for meeting again never materialized. Ken and Neil, wherever you are, my thanks for building my self-confidence!

While I was at Ruth's, my father called to say that he and Mother had decided to accept an urgent invitation to join the faculty at Oregon State College. After his address there three years earlier, he had been asked back as the keynote speaker for an important conference and since that time had been besieged with offers to move west to the campus. Professionally and personally, he felt that it was time to leave Arkansas. He wondered if I had met any young women from the University of Oregon or Oregon State at the conference. Perhaps if I could make such contacts, they would ease my way when we moved west. I was shocked that what he had mentioned, almost in passing, as a possibility had become a real course of action. And yet as I heard the excitement in his voice and remembered that I had met a sorority sister from the University of Oregon just the day before, the spark of adventure lodged in me and I could anticipate what lay ahead.

When I got home I found a great storm of agitation aroused by my father's resignation. The Board of Trustees called a special meeting after President Futrall's offers of a marked salary increase failed to change Daddy's mind. Even the Governor was called in to make a special plea. Daddy remained firm. The family knew that what he felt courtesy demanded he fail to say was that he had decided that certain Southern cultural attitudes regarding race and class made him want to move his family to a more liberal environment. We were truly going to take the Oregon trail. Charles and I talked endlessly about what this move would mean for us and could only wait and see.

## Watching Him Run

The May air slipped like silk around me as I stepped from a shower onto the soft bath mat. All was body temperature and I hardly needed the leisurely swish of a towel before I could powder and put on panties, a bra and half-slip, then the white one-piece silk printed in small bright signal flags. It tied at the waist with a narrow self-belt, and this was its first wearing. Light, released, I stretched in pleasure. I was eighteen and this was spring!

As I brushed my hair and rolled it in the back, I looked critically in the mirror—and was satisfied with what I saw. This was unusual because I could often find something in my appearance to object to—my eyebrows were too heavy and I didn't like plucking, my mouth was too big, my breasts were too small. But today all was well. My hair was freshly washed and shining, my summer tan was well on its way. I really liked being thin and taller than most of my friends. I put on my watch and realized that I had to move right along or be late to the track meet. No chance for a ride—Charles was running. I would join friends from the house at the track.

In less than a month I would be graduating. Later in the summer we would be moving west—to Oregon. What would the West be like? Ever since my parents had made the decision to leave Arkansas for the Pacific Northwest, I had wondered. Charles and I found no answers. He was a junior, headed for a law career in his father's office in Jonesboro. My excitement about graduating was threatened by my anxiety over leaving Charles, leaving Arkansas, leaving the life I knew so well and loved so much.

By now I was at the track, heading for the bleachers and looking for someone I knew to sit with. That silken air still played between my body and my clothes. The sun was warm but a breeze lifted my hair. "Hey-O, Margaret!" I heard the call and then a whistle, knew that girls from the house were there. Sure enough— close to the middle and near the top with room for me that they had saved. I scrambled up to sit with two of my best friends—one of them had a beau on the track team, too.

We laughed and gossiped about the meet and our chances against SMU, the dance coming up that night, who was being "pinned" and whose pin was being returned. Some whistles blew, a few cheers rallied the stands, (after all, this wasn't football!) and the contest was under way. I had searched the field for Charles' handsome black head and finally found it. He had seen me and we exchanged our private sign. Now I had to wait for what was, to me, the main event. Charles was a 440 man, a quarter-miler. This race is not everybody's favorite. It doesn't have the flash and the immediacy of the sprints and hurdles. It doesn't display the dogged endurance of the distance races. But it does have its own timing and rhythm—speed off the blocks to establish pace and place, the classic run in the middle of the race when on most tracks the runners seem to position themselves in a nearly uniform stride, and then the demanding sprint at the end. It is a beautiful race to watch and a hard race to run.

They were on the track. Charles had drawn a good lane, second from the inside, between two runners, one so blond and pale and seemingly fragile that his finishing any race seemed doubtful. Two other Arkansas men drew outside lanes. They all dug into their blocks, worked their spikes into good position, dropped down over their feet. Then the call, "On your mark—Get set," brought them up tense and ready for the gun. It was a good start. Charles ran easily and took advantage of his position. As they rounded the track and appeared in mid-race to be running almost singly, Charles drew ahead. He was a natural runner with an easy open stride. But right on his heels came SMU's blond challenger, and he stayed right there matching Charles stride for stride. They came around into the finishing sprint almost shoulder to shoulder. As they neared the tape, first one seemed to be ahead, then the other. I screamed, "Go, Charles!" just as the deceptively fragile blond lunged with his SMU jersey a fraction of an inch— but all that was needed—ahead of Charles' red Razorback chest. They stumbled off the track into clumps of waiting teammates, either exultant or commiserating. I blinked the tears out of my eyes—it had been such a beautiful day.

## Graduation and Farewell

I was so caught up in the fever of pre-graduation activity that I could hardly spend time wondering about the future. I had discovered dance in my junior year and was rehearsing and performing in two all-campus programs. The titles tell a great deal about the times—in "The Sun and Earth's Awakening," I danced the Spirit of the Waves, draped in tie-dyed blue and green crepe de chine, and as the Matchmaker in "A Russian Yarmark" I supported an immense lace headdress and clicked high red boots. It all became so important to me that I decided to make dancing my career, abandoning my four year English major. My parents, bless them, urged me to think about it carefully but made no objection. They had probably seen it coming.

Incidental to my dance commitment were the part I took in a Lambda Tau play, "The Old Signor," and an appearance as Salome in an exhibit of Living Pictures. I must have lived forty-eight hour days that spring.

During my last three years at the university, I had lived part time at the house and part time at home. Now that my time in school was growing short, Mother and Daddy were generous enough to entertain the whole sorority at a farewell luncheon. It was sort of a Last Hurrah, in my mind.

As time hurtled on toward graduation, my feelings and, I am sure, those of my family became more complex. There were so many farewells that everything seemed to have a for-the-last-time air about it. The heady exhilaration of being ready to graduate with a satisfactory scholastic record was mixed with outright fear of a graduate year in Oregon. (My parents had issued an outright order on this score: I was to be at home, going to Oregon State to meet people my age for the first year in a new state.)

Mother and Daddy were widely feted. They were a popular couple and everyone they knew wanted to do something for them. After each affair they came home bearing gifts that spoke of the affection in which they were held. How they managed the goodbyes and the thank yous with such grace, I found hard to understand. Only Jimmie, thirteen, and just starting high school appeared to handle the departure quietly. He saw his regular pals daily with no fuss, muss, or bother.

Finally—the beautiful June day of the commencement ceremonies. The platform had been erected in front of Old Main under towering oaks and maples. Tiers of chairs and bleachers swept in an arc facing it. There was the customary place for everyone and everyone was in place. The trustees, President Futrall, the faculty, the graduates, their beaming families and assorted friends and students marched in the academic procession or sat watching the ritual. The stage was set for the most dramatic part of the day—my father was awarded an honorary doctor of laws degree by a grateful university he had served for fourteen years. Tears clouded my eyes, rolled down my cheeks. Otis Jernigan, seated next to me by an inexorable alphabet, handed me an immaculate large white handkerchief. I could see Mother over in the faculty family section resorting to my same tactics.

There were few enough of us in a graduating class of just under two hundred so that we each had our turn at mounting and crossing the platform, receiving a diploma and congratulations with a warm handshake, flipping our tassels to the proper side of our mortar boards and returning to our seats. I stood alone to receive honors—graduation, class and departmental in English and education. I was also awarded a teaching certificate, which seemed a bit anticlimactic. The long four years had gone by so fast!

Mother and Daddy went off to faculty festivities. Charles and I joined some other couples, all of us a trifle sad over necessary partings and fathomless futures.

There was one more celebratory event to come. Daddy had been Director of the Summer Session for a good many years and had agreed to stay on for this final year. At the customary Farewell Convocation, held in the same grassy spot where graduation had taken place, he had concluded the short program with a brief valedictory, full of the emotion he felt at leaving. As the audience stood, cheering and applauding, a committee of students crossed the lawn in front of the platform. "Just a minute, Dean Jewell," they said and stood either side of their dear faculty friend and mentor while a long blue Buick coach was driven up between audience and platform. Out popped Ben Winkelman, the student driver, who handed my astonished father the set of car keys. Pandemonium reigned! This magnificent gift from the students who had loved him so greatly was to carry us to Oregon.

Only five days later, my father spent his last day in the Peabody Hall office where he had given so much of himself during our life in Arkansas. The following five days were spent in packing boxes, crating furniture, preparing to leave the Hill Street house, Fayetteville, and Arkansas for our Western adventure. A freight car was loaded with our furniture, trunks and boxes, and we spent a couple of nights with neighborhood friends. We were to be ready to leave early in the morning of July 25, 1927.

True to my grandmother's saying when life seemed to go off the track, "Man proposes, God disposes," we were not able to drive away. Jimmie, true to form, became very ill in the middle of the night and had to be taken to City Hospital. His soaring fever and blood tests indicating pneumonia or appendicitis prompted Dr. Ellis to call three doctors in consultation. One, a specialist from Kansas City, pronounced it pylitis. By whatever diagnosis, Jimmie was critically ill. His temperature hovered at one hundred four degrees or above for five days before plunging far below normal. Why surgery was not performed, I have no idea.

We were in limbo. Mother and Daddy spent most of their time at the hospital. I visited once or twice each day and wandered for hours at our empty house trying to feel at home again. Friends housed us, fed us, strengthened us. And Jimmie got better, remarkably fast after such a crisis. He was allowed to come "home" after two or three days without fever. Friends moved some furniture back into the house and we camped there as Jimmie gained strength.

Finally, a little less than two weeks after our planned departure, my father drove our heavily packed car, a thin white son and a sobbing daughter out of Fayetteville and into the future. Mother provided necessary continuity with her customary cry as we backed down the driveway, "Ralph, Ralph, wait a minute. Stop the car! I've lost my purse." This was the usual prelude to all our trips. The purse was found on the floor of the car—also as usual—and we were on our way.

## My Arkansas Homes

A dozen years ago in 1977, I returned to Fayetteville, Arkansas, where I had lived from the time I was four until I was eighteen. Fayetteville, the Athens of the Ozarks, according to the Chamber of Commerce billing, was the scene of my growing up, and I was going back for the first time since I had left it for the West Coast. The occasion was the first and, so far as I know, the only reunion of Peabody School, the small, experimental school on the University of Arkansas campus, which I had attended until I entered college—still on the same campus.

It was to be a total reunion—of all the graduates—and as the small Frontier plane dipped over the green studded limestone of the Ozarks for its landing, I wondered how many people might attend. Two hundred, two fifty, I thought. That would certainly be a generous estimate. Who would it include?

That estimate was a poor one. There were more than seven hundred happy souls milling around in the largest, newest exhibit hall of the Washington County Fairgrounds, rented to accomodate the unexpected crowd. In addition to members of my class and those above and below me, there were men and women who had represented age and sophistication to me when I was growing up. Bill Fulbright, distinguished senator from Arkansas, and his older sister, Lucile, were two of these. The Fulbright twins, younger than Bill, were my contemporaries. And there were many "little" sisters and brothers of my friends, considered beneath my notice in earlier years, who had somehow turned into amazingly personable men and women since my departure.

It was fun to catch the eye of Edgar Sommers, who had become the undertaker he had hoped to be as a boy, and laughingly recall the hazardous games of crack-the-whip, our favorite neighborhood sport, including the time I got cracked from the end of the serpentine line and flew off the terrace to land in the street against the curb. "God protects children and drunks," we decided. I had been too young to have the protection of alcohol.

It was disconcerting to have one of my classmates question me as we skated on the thin conversational ice of being supposed to remember one another and she looked hard at my name tag, "Margaret Jewell? Were you any relation to Dean Jewell?"

I felt as though I had been rescued from quicksand and was again on solid ground. "Yes," I replied happily, "a very close relative. He was my father."

She looked doubtfully at my white hair, put out her hand about the level of my elbow, and said skeptically, "Oh, but you were a little girl with long brown curls!"

Such skepticism was overpowering. I glanced down toward her gesture, wondering if I had really come. . .

That same wonder was reinforced by the frequent question, "What did you think when you went by to see your house?" Actually, I had not had time to try to see any of the three houses we had lived in during our fourteen years in Fayetteville, because an emergency had made me a day late in arrival. I had barely made it to the reunion proper. But the following morning I began my pilgrimage on foot, refusing as gracefully as I could the friendly offers to drive me here and there. I wanted to walk to my homes as if I were coming home from school.

Leverett Street was closest to the campus, only a long block uphill from the marble steps that had led toward Peabody Hall, where my father's offices were on the top floor and Peabody School occupied the ground floor. The Department of Home Economics, where in seventh grade I had taken Cooking and Sewing, had held forth in the basement.

Crossing the street, I started up the short, steep hill toward my first home in Arkansas. It was down that hill I had coasted my first time on two skates, a sawed-off broomstick between my legs as a brake. Dismayed at my slow descent, I had closed my eyes, remembering that when we were driving it felt much faster when my eyes were shut. Coming home from the campus, my father had seen me gather speed as I clutched my broomstick and veer sharply off the high curb into the gutter. It was paved in those times with cut sandstone that left a nasty gash.

On up the hill I went, past Miss Bunker's small house, still painted brown, then on to our next-door neighbor, Mrs. Richardson's severe early Victorian. It had been recently restored in shades of dove gray with immaculate white trim. The big maples I used to climb separated her house from—but where was ours? The only one-story house I ever lived in until I came to California, white, wide-verandaed, a broad porch swing at the side under the wisteria—it was gone. Totally gone. Nothing in its place. The quarter of a block on which it had stood was now a small park, only luxuriant turf and spreading trees. The rose garden was there, but the barn on whose roof I liked to perch had been razed. I was startled, looked quickly across the street to see the Harding's house still there. It was on the high side of the neatly paved street. The sandy ruts in the old street used to run red as old blood after a rain. In summer the horse-drawn ice cream wagon jingled down Leverett Street, stopping to offer, "Vanilla, chocolate, strawberry?" How dared they destroy my home?

After walking around the grassy park, I turned back toward the campus, down the skating hill and up the marble steps. I would cross in front of Old Main, past the Chemistry and Engineering buildings, out beyond the new stadium, and be on my way to Hill Street, our last home before we moved to Oregon. It was a walk of more than two miles in the late May sunshine, and it gave me lots of time to think and to remember.

Downhill I went and through the hollow where a small creek once ran between clumps of willow and wild cherry. Grass had grown tall there and wild iris blossomed early in the spring. New houses, well-manicured lawns, and formal gardens filled the hollow and featured creekside plantings. I walked slowly, marveling at the changed landscape.

Up the hill toward the old neighborhood, I saw where the Dunns had lived, across from the Cates and around the corner from the Ripleys. The Cates' wide lawns had made room for two new houses, smaller but attractive. What would 31 Hill Street look like? Would the big barn turned garage still be there? I remembered the litter of mongrel puppies we had found under the rough planks of the floor—five whimpering squirmers who demonstrated their mother's catholic taste in mates. We kept homely little Frisk, who took care of her beautiful but feeble-minded littermate, ineptly named Flash. (A feeble-minded dog is a truly pitiable beast—poor Flash couldn't find his food bowl without help.)

I hurried on, half-expecting to see Will Carr out by the smokehouse or at work in the big vegetable garden of which he was so proud. He grew the best Country Gentleman corn I have ever tasted, and his pickling cucumbers were something special. Perhaps Mrs. Donnelly would come to the door, keening over her latest grief. I rounded the corner, hoping for a sundrenched sniff of heavy fragrance from the honeysuckle screen opposite the cistern. But before my eyes rose a large, three-story apartment complex. Built with wide spreading wings, it made the most of the spacious lot—again a quarter of a block. That it was a notably attractive building pleased me. The tall elm that held my bag swing was gone, of course, but many of the maples remained. The four o'clocks that curled so neatly around my fingers when their seed pods were popped had disappeared, as had the iris beds, in favor of designed plantings, low shrubs, bright annuals, colorful and orderly. The brick path with its ricrac edging, on which I regularly fell and cut parallel slashes in my knees, had been replaced by a wide, sweeping concrete walkway with a flat brick trim.

Handsome and impersonal, this was no longer my home. It had been to this Hill Street house that our family, diminished to four, had returned broken-hearted after Baby Keith's death in Tennessee.

I felt no need to wander about the complex, no wish to confront my memories with the realities of the present day. The sprawling white house across the corner, where the nuns had lived one summer, was gone. They used to practice tennis strokes on the front lawn, looking like giant black moths with habits tucked up in their belts out of the swing of their racquets. Excavation showed where another apartment compound would probably rise before long. Down the hill I went toward the cemetery, a favorite trysting place; blue periwinkle running over the gentle mounds made the headstones seem to float in a sea of vines. Locust trees just coming into bloom arched over the graves. The lilacs had faded but honeysuckle and roses and the silver-white syringa blended fragrance. Catalpa bonnets would blossom in time for Children's Day in June. My skin priclked with gooseflesh when I remembered Chuck, with whom I had spent many hours here, now lying at peace under his own headstone. My heart missed a beat.

Down into another hollow and up another hill (Fayetteville, like Athens, was built on seven hills) around the corner by the Kappa Sig house and I was at the campus end of Dickson Street. I could walk slowly east through Shulertown, past the railroad station, check out the small business community clustered there and be at 223 Dickson Street, the home about which most of my memories of growing up—to the advanced age of thirteen—center.

I wished that there were time to stop at Tony's for a cherry coke poured over a glass filled with finely flaked ice or a nut sundae swimming in syrup. Would those long ago treats still be there for the asking? Of the three grocery stores: Bates Brothers, Gollaher's, and the one that had the best dill pickles—enormous and swimming in a barrel of brine—only one remained, and it sported an unknown name. The bank was still there, looking more prosperous than I remembered. The hardware store seemed smaller, less forbidding, and the U of A Cafe was gone—what delectable dinners we had had there on Sundays after church when Elizabeth was gone for the day. My father used to love to imitate the middle-aged waitress who always asked, "Roast beef, roast pork, or smothered chicken?" Daddy implied (out of her hearing) that the unfortunate bird had met a wretched death. Camera shops, beauty salons, real estate offices competed for space on Dickson Street, but I was not prepared for what I saw on the corner where our home had stood.

In its time, a spreading two-story house, wrapped around with a broad veranda on which we were permitted to skate, it stood high on its terrace, separated from the sidewalk by a formal wall of large cut-stone blocks. Big old trees surrounded it. There were candlabra yuccas by the corner fence, flowering shrubs and rose bushes, holly-hocks and clematis, jasmine and honey-suckle. My play-house, the old servants' quarters, and the barn separated the big house from the vegetable garden, the beehives, and the stableyard. I could have found my way around either house or garden blindfolded—except that they were gone. Truly gone. The quarter block lot had been bulldozed to street level, a good-sized parking lot, macadam-paved, was filled with cars that stood waiting for their owners, who were presumably shopping inside the large, well-lighted cut-rate liquor store. Advertising banners on the windows proclaimed bargain prices for Jack Daniels, Southern Comfort, Early Times, and Budweiser Beer. How glad I was that my mother wasn't with me to feel the shock. A lifetime teetotaler, born and bred in the dry state of Kansas, she would have felt it incumbent on her to become a latter-day Carrie Nation. My father would have brought his quick wit to the rescue—not Mother. She would have been shamed, saddened.

My own heart beat to a heavier rhythm. I had fantasized a visit to this special Mecca and had hoped that an understanding resident would invite me in when I rang the bell and introduced myself. The reunion's "little girl with long brown curls" desperately wanted to step inside the front door, peer up the curving stairway down which she had fallen after Violet's push and then turn to the right and, crossing the entry, go into the front parlor. The player piano would no longer stand there for her to pump for hours as the rolls of music from the bulging cabinet were carefully selected and hooked onto the turning roller. Everything from "K-K-K-Katie" to "Georgia Camp Meeting," from "Humoresque" to the Triumphal March from "Aida" had rung through the house as she pedaled faster to accelerate, slowed to a largo, manipulated the proper levers to achieve a thundering fortissimo in the "Turkish March" or a quiet piano for the "Moonlight Sonata." Practicing had never been fun, especially with the fear of Frau Schmidt's ruler cracking her knuckles for a misplayed note, but the creation of music possible on the player piano was sheer heaven.

Just as that little girl with dark curls achieved virtuosity on the keyboard, she had felt herself one with Alma Gluck, Madame Schumann-Heink, Louise Homer, and even the Great Caruso when she played their heavy records on the domed Victrola that stood across the room between the windows.

The back parlor, through two open arches, one on either side of the double fireplace, had held the bookcases, tier on tier, the treasures within protected by leaded glass that lowered or slid back on metal brackets. She had had free access to all the books, and it was on the bottom shelf of the stack nearest the front parlor that she had discovered the small brown German primer and set out to teach herself the language. Her parents had studied German in school and used it occasionally for private comments after she had passed the point of being able to grasp the meaning of spelled words. This new skill would be her secret. Already she could read the first words—it was an alphabet! Helped by the engraved illustration of her favorite fruit, she read, "apfel," printed in a strange, sharp-cornered script. The excitement of true scholarly research inflamed her zeal. Day after day she pulled the primer from the shelf, but the going was hard. There was only one "apfel" and the Old German script was decorative but illegible to her. She was not, to put it mildly, a born linguist.

The back parlor had been transformed into a hospital room when Mother came home from the local sanitorium with the promised new baby, a tiny sister, Keith. The birth unfortunately coincided with the disastrous flu epidemic of 1919, and Dr. Ellis felt that a degree of protection and better nursing could be achieved at home than at the beleaguered hospital. Mother fell ill but Keith was untouched by the flu. However, my brother Jimmie, who always was desperately sick, had pneumonia, and hung for days between life and death. A bed was made for him in the back parlor, and my father and Elizabeth went on twenty-four hour nursing duty with the help of a practical nurse who came in daily. Where is Elizabeth now, I wondered. Did she go back to her sweetheart, Jerd, in the mountains? Did she have children? Grandchildren? She had been such a vital part of Dickson Street.

It had been December when Keith was born, much too cold to seek the solace of the screened porch off my room, where I lay in summer daydreaming as in a treehouse. Two years after her birth, I read the whole Bible through during the months of summer vacation. My grandmother urged the effort on me, reinforcing her request with an offer of a fifteen dollar reward for the Old Testament and ten dollars for the New—very big money for those days. She showed real feeling for the difference in length and difficulty of the two chronicles. I can easily bring back the feeling of holding the small violet volume above my eyes as I lay propped on pillows and felt the summer call to me through the fine screening.

Try as hard as I could, I could never recover Dickson Street. The feel of the smooth siding on my playhouse as I climbed the narrow outside stairs to its second-story fastness made my fingers throb in memory. The look and smell of the dust motes when I opened the door to fantasy lived on in my mind alone. I turned toward the hill, whose steep street crossed Dickson at the corner where Jimmie had dug his surprise fortress. Sailing down that hill on skates or bicycle had been my delight, my mother's despair. Braking was not always easy at the bottom, and one had to be wary of cars and trucks before flying out into traffic. The Liebolt's boarding house stood on that corner across from us. Fred Liebolt, the worst tease in town, is now an internationally known New York surgeon. Perhaps if I walked away from Dickson Street and up the hill, I would pass Irene Gollaher's yellow house with the sprawling Cecil Bruner rosebush. And at the top of the hill on Mt. Nord, I'd see the Fulbright home, the old Arkansas Building from the St. Louis Exposition before my time. From its Greek Revival eminence, I could look down over Fayetteville and say goodbye to my three homes.